CONTENTS

INTRODUCTION

Yes, you should read this.

"Back home, I was curious about Jesus, but didn't have the chance to learn. Now that I'm here, I can! Can we get coffee and talk?"
- A newly arrived international student

We live in an amazing time for connecting with Muslim international students!

In the past few decades, Muslims are coming to faith in Jesus like never before seen. For many of them, the journey involves dreams and visions from the Lord, answered prayers, and miraculous signs. Paraphrasing Jesus' own words, many witnesses who have gone before us longed to see what we are seeing today but did not see it (Matthew 13:17). God is drawing people to himself from all corners of the earth.

In the past few decades, more Muslim international students have come to study in the West than ever before. Countries send us their best and brightest, the future leaders of industry, culture, and politics. While they are here, there is a short window for them to build positive relationships with Christians that can overwrite our religions' rocky history and open up conversations that for many, like the student quoted above, have been desired but unattainable. They are here, and they are curious.

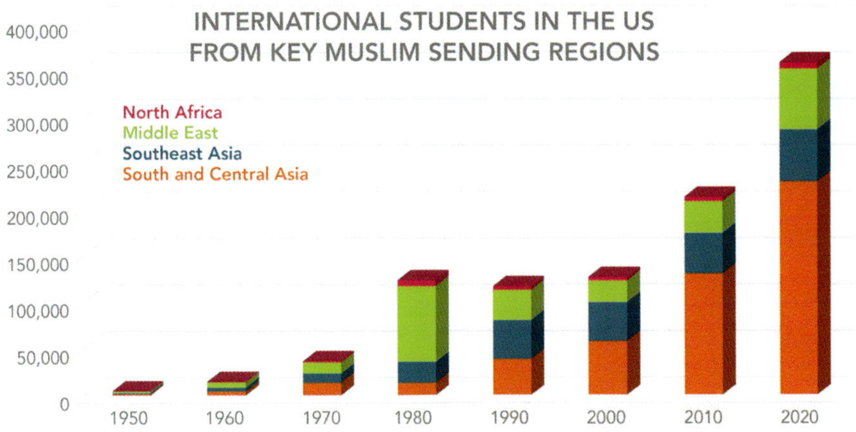

In the past few decades, our own Western cultures have grown less religious and more intolerant of faith. It is often difficult for Christian students to find peers who want to talk about spiritual matters. In this climate, Muslims stand alongside us as fellow religious sojourners, seeking to honor God and live according to his plan. They are refreshingly eager to converse with us about the topics we hold dear: both where we have common ground and where we differ significantly.

There has never been a better time for befriending Muslims in Jesus' name.

▶ WHAT IS THIS?

This handbook gathers the best material from our international student ministry, organized and abbreviated into a simple guide for you. We have written primarily with Christian college students in mind, both those who are just getting started and those who already have experience with Muslims. We have attempted to be concise while doing justice to these important topics. You will learn some history, theology, sociology, and anthropology because we need to be informed to minister with wisdom and sensitivity. We also want to be practical. You will learn many specific ideas, conversation topics, events and ministry plans.

▶ WHO WROTE IT?

It takes a village… The primary author, Paul, was assisted with ideas, stories, and editing by a ministry team made up of women and men, Americans and internationals, including one Christ-follower from a Muslim background. Combined we have upwards of 100 years of experience serving Muslims in the US and internationally. What that means is we have made a *lot* of mistakes and can try to help you do better!

▶ SHOULD I READ IT ALL?

As any author would say, "Yes! Thou shalt read every single page." But we get it: you're really busy. This handbook follows a logical progression with each chapter building on the previous. However, if a particular chapter looks most interesting or relevant to where you're at, jump in there first.

If you picked this handbook up at the beginning of the semester and you're ready to get started immediately, solo or as part of a team, jump to chapter 9 first. That chapter will help you make a plan and begin building relationships on campus.

Our suggestion? Read this handbook with a group of friends, taking time to pray and discuss each chapter, and *acting* on the things you read as you go.

Here is what's ahead:

- Chapter 1 gives inspiration and principles for interfaith ministry from Jesus' own life.
- Chapter 2 unpacks some of the origins of Islam and the often-rocky history of Christians and Muslims together.
- Chapter 3 draws out common threads of Muslim identity to help you understand your friends' cultures and values.
- Chapter 4 gets into how to build friendships with Muslims while centralizing faith.
- Chapter 5 has tips and plans for studying the Bible with Muslims, or the Bible and the Qur'an side by side.
- Chapter 6 looks at the ways many Muslims come to follow Jesus, with guidance for explaining the gospel and decisions.
- Chapter 7 covers walking alongside new believers in discipleship.
- Chapter 8 discusses how international students can return home well.
- Chapter 9 provides a framework for building campus plans.

There is so much more to be said on every topic in this handbook, and everything you read here is built on the work of many others who have guided us. When relevant, we give suggestions for where you can read more. We also would love to hear from you at paulforrester@intervarsity.org. Share questions or feedback, and let us know how you

are connecting with Muslim international students. We are your teammates in that wonderful calling, and we are praying for you.

▶ A NOTE TO MUSLIMS READING THIS HANDBOOK:

Salaam alaykum, friends! We are honored that you hold this book in your hands. While our primary audience is Christian college students, you are welcome to read through these pages as well. There are two values that guide our connections with Muslims: we want to be respectful, and we want to be clear.

First, we want to respect and honor Muslims with the ways we describe you, your cultures, and your faith. We have been deeply blessed by Muslims who are our friends, students, teachers, babysitters, colleagues, and family members, from all around the world. We hope that the words in this handbook treat you honorably and fairly.

Second, we want to be clear. We are followers of *Isa al Masih*, Jesus the Messiah. We believe that he offers life, truth, peace, forgiveness, and hope like none other, and that he offers it to all. It is our sincere hope that you and everyone else in the world will meet the real Jesus, and so we write openly and persuasively about our faith. Our own Muslim friends are equally passionate about sharing their faith with us! This is true friendship, so may we continue to share our beliefs, and may God lead us all into his truth.

Happy reading!

Paul Forrester and the CWMIS writing team
paulforrester@intervarsity.org

1 FOLLOWING JESUS' EXAMPLE

So he left Judea and went back once more to Galilee. Now he had to go through Samaria. So he came to a town in Samaria called Sychar, near the plot of ground Jacob had given to his son Joseph. Jacob's well was there, and Jesus, tired as he was from the journey, sat down by the well. It was about noon. When a Samaritan woman came to draw water, Jesus said to her, "Will you give me a drink?"

John 4:3-7 (NIV)

Alejandra wasn't sure what to expect when visiting her new friend Fatima. Their few conversations on campus had been enjoyable but generally superficial, so when Fatima invited Alejandra to stop by for tea, she knew things were going to a new level. Fatima opened the door while still tucking one last curl of black hair under her hijab. But when she saw that Alejandra was the only guest, she removed the headscarf entirely. Taking her cue from the pile of shoes by the door, Alejandra removed her own. A brief fear of smelly socks flashed through her mind but passed when Fatima presented her with a pair of simple spa-style slippers "for inside use."

> Over the following three hours the two chatted about everything from extended family (like Fatima's Saudi family, Alejandra's Chilean family was tight knit with three generations living together) to favorite foods (Who knew jello was not *halal*,[1] permissible?) to prayer (Fatima prefers reciting memorized prayers in the mosque, Alejandra spontaneous ones during musical worship). Two of Fatima's neighbors invited themselves in and were welcome additions to the conversation. At one point Alejandra asked about the artfully framed Qur'anic verse on the wall. It was reminiscent of something Jesus taught. When Alejandra finally left and began the walk home, she was surprised to find herself simultaneously exhausted and invigorated.

How in the world do we start ministry with Muslims? We look to Jesus! In John 4 we have a portrait of interfaith ministry between the Jewish Messiah and a Samaritan outcast. Their meeting has a number of parallels to Christians connecting with Muslim international students. Like Alejandra, we will bump into differences and discover similarities to our own traditions and practices.

Note the following choices our Lord made as he interacted with the woman, which we will also face with Muslims. Each of these concepts will be unpacked in the coming chapters. By following his example, our ministry with Muslims will be on sure footing.

APPROACHING DIFFERENCES DIAGRAM

Responding well to cultural differences opens the door to relationships

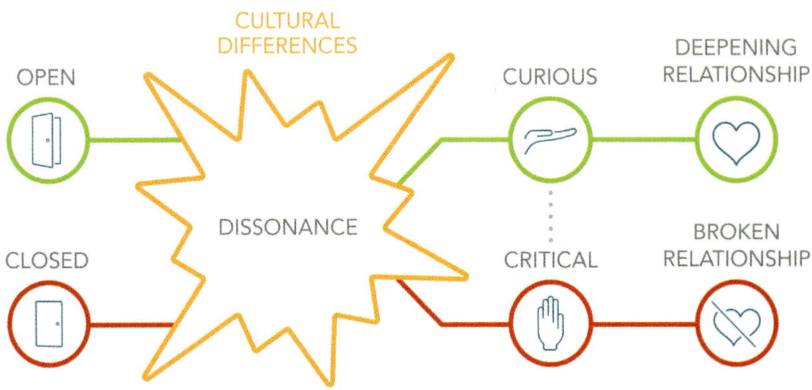

SEE A 4-MINUTE VIDEO EXPLANATION tiny.cc/a-d

FACING OUR MESSY HISTORY

Jesus and the Samaritan woman had a past—not them personally, but the groups they came from and represented. There had been hundreds of years of tension and even atrocities. Jews destroyed the Samaritan temple in 113 BC. Samaritans scattered bones in the Jewish Temple during Passover around 6 AD. A few decades after Jesus' resurrection, in AD 52, a group of Samaritans massacred Jewish pilgrims, which was met by a reprisal Jewish raid.[2] You better believe that history mattered whenever these two groups met.

Muslims and Christians have been interacting for 1,400 years. There have been friendships, honest dialogues, and moments of positive cooperation for the common good, but also times of misunderstanding, tragedy, and violence. As with the news, it is usually the bad stories that make headlines and are remembered. Some tragedies, like the Crusades, happened explicitly in the name of religion. Others are the product of our politics but are viewed through the lens of religion because for most Muslims the West and Christianity are synonymous.

When Jesus approached the Samaritan woman, he was well aware of the history that separated them. Likewise, we must learn the history of our faiths' interactions, including facing the sins and misdeeds done by many bearing the banner of Christ. Learning and responding to this history is the topic of chapter 2.

RECOGNIZING POWER DYNAMICS

A man had explicitly higher status than a woman in the first century and unmarried men and women did not spend time together. The fact that the Samaritan woman visited the well alone at midday instead of with other women in the morning likely shows she was an outcast, too. No wonder she was surprised that Jesus would start up a conversation. It's fair to say that were this meeting to go awry and word get back to her town, she would bear still more blame and shame.

Jesus is aware of the power imbalance between them but navigates it with gentleness. He puts himself in a position of need by requesting water from her. And when he addresses her rocky past with other men, he does it in a context of offering her a tremendous gift. This humble woman is privileged as one of the first to learn the identity of the Messiah, the one who "will explain everything to us" (John 4:25).

Even if you are subordinated in other areas of life, you likely hold power when interacting with Muslim international students on Western campuses.

How do different aspects of your identity (gender, ethnicity, background, economic status, and so on) affect the power you hold? Even if you are subordinated in other areas of life, you likely hold power when interacting with Muslim international students on Western campuses. Is English your native language? Do people in this country generally assume your religion is normal? You are meeting in a society shaped by Christian thinking and values, in a country that has since 9/11 been suspicious of women in hijabs and men with dark beards. Do you have US citizenship? Living here on student visas, Muslim internationals can be deported quickly. And the fact that they are far from their home culture and community means you are only experiencing a small slice of their identity. There are plenty of reasons for international students to keep their heads down and avoid drawing attention.

Considering these power dynamics will help you approach Muslims with the sensitivity that comes from awareness, like Jesus did. And if you are privileged enough to visit a Muslim-majority country you will experience the role reversal and see the richness of your friends' cultures in full color. Chapter 3 will help you understand Muslim people and cultures so you can engage sensitively.

▶ GOING OUT OF OUR WAY

Jesus crossed both geographic and cultural barriers to reach this woman. The account in John 4 tells us that he "had to go through Samaria" (v.2), but if you look at a first century map you will see another option. Many pilgrims on the same journey chose to travel the long way, around Samaria, to avoid the other ethno-religious group. Viewing each other as heretics

Mosaic of Jesus and the woman at the well in the Church of the Savior on Spilled Blood in St. Petersburg, Russia

and resenting each other for historical wrongs, it is no surprise that, as John succinctly put it, Jews did not associate with Samaritans. Jesus knew exactly what he was doing when he guided the disciples to Jacob's well that day. He "*had* to go through Samaria" because he was determined to find this precious woman and offer living water that would quench her deepest need.

It's unlikely today that you could live your entire life without meeting a Muslim person. But it's quite possible for an American Christian student never to build a friendship with a Muslim international student. Many if not the majority of international students in the US never have the chance to visit an American home. And just as Samaritans were not likely to hang out at Jewish cultural events, most Muslim internationals will not voluntarily show up at Christian events. So if that is where you spend all your time, you may miss Samaria. Don't do it!

Rather than building an attractional ("come to our turf") ministry only, aim for an incarnational ("go be among them") approach. Alejandra did this when she entered Fatima's home. And like Alejandra, get ready for cultural differences. Chapter 4 discusses how to go out of your way to find and build gospel friendships with Muslims on campus.

▶ NAVIGATING "CLOSE-BUT-NOT-THE-SAME" RELIGION

Jesus crossed theological barriers, too. Samaritan religion was similar to Judaism but there were some clear departures. Samaritans worshiped the same God but regarded only the Pentateuch as Scripture. Their temple had been on Mt. Gerizim rather than in Jerusalem, as the woman reminded Jesus. Jews considered themselves the true children of Jacob and viewed Samaritans as half-breeds.

If you have spent time in dialogue with Muslims, you are aware of the similarities between our faiths. We both worship one God, respect Abraham as a patriarch, believe in angels and demons, hope for the afterlife, and more. Fellowship with other believers, and disciplines such as prayer and fasting are important to us. In a spiritual conversation with a Muslim, a Hindu, and an atheist you'll find an immediate ally in the Muslim.

But you also have likely bumped—or crashed—into theological differences. Muslims honor Jesus as a great prophet and miracle worker, but the idea of a "Son of God" is immensely challenging to them. We both believe in a version of sin, falling short of God's standard, but differ on the depth of the problem and how it affects the world.

Being "cousins" of similar faiths is exciting at first but also may lead to talking past each other because we incorrectly assume that concepts have the same meaning on both sides. Chapter 5 has tips and detailed plans for constructive Bible study so Muslims can learn our faith from the source.

▶ PLAYING OUR PART IN THE CONVERSION PROCESS

When in verse 28 the woman abandons her water jar and rushes back to her village, how much does she know about following Christ? Precious little! But enough to plant the seed of transformation in her. She has had a personal encounter with the Messiah who knows her heart. She's experienced how being loved and graciously accepted changes everything, and she is overjoyed.

Most Muslims who come to faith in Christ journey through a lengthy process marked by significant moments. God is sending many Muslims dreams and visions of Jesus. There may be an answered prayer or a powerful experience of the Spirit's presence. Or they may be captivated by Jesus through studying the Bible. They eventually come to a point of surrendering to Jesus as Savior and Lord.

Their identity in Christ will be worked out on the journey of discipleship, with the Holy Spirit to guide.

Yet there are unresolved questions about their theology, their community and future, and even what exactly to call themselves (Christian? Follower of *Isa*?). Each of these questions was present for the woman at the well, too. In fact, the Scriptures are full of characters who are transformed through a relatively brief encounter with Christ or his followers. Their identity in him will be worked out on the journey of discipleship, with the Holy Spirit to guide. Likewise in ministry with Muslims we must treat the discipleship process as equally important to the decision moment. Chapter 6 will help you understand our part in this key moment, and chapter 7 covers how to walk alongside new believers in the journey of discipleship.

SENDING MISSIONARIES TO THEIR OWN

Both the woman at the well in John 4 and the Gerasene demoniac (Mark 5) were non-Jews who came to faith. In both settings, rather than inviting them to journey onward with his tribe of followers, Jesus blessed them to go and tell others about him. They became missionaries to their own communities, because who could be better to share the gospel message of God's inbreaking kingdom!

This, too, is the ultimate hope and prayer of international student ministry: that students who meet Christ while abroad will return to share with their families and communities. Many Muslim international students and scholars come from countries closed to the gospel, with extremely few believers. They are by far the least-reached people on campus. Maybe God will use

you to send disciples who will make disciples around the world. Chapter 8 will show you how to prepare them to return with faith that can not simply survive back home, but also deepen and spread.

They became missionaries to their own communities, because who could be better to share the gospel message!

▶ FINDING JOYFUL MINISTRY

The woman sprints away from the well so fast that she forgets her water jug. "Come, see a man who told me everything I ever did!" (John 4:30). When someone is ready to proclaim their deepest sins, you know they are excited. The TV series *The Chosen* has a beautiful reenactment of this scene and portrays not just her but Jesus grinning in sheer enjoyment.[3]

"Ministry with Muslims is..." How would you complete that sentence? For myself and many others, the answers are "...refreshing," "...faith-deepening," "...a joy." It is exhilarating to talk with people who are ready and eager to have spiritual conversations, as most Muslims are. Our faith grows when we consider their thoughtful questions and see them discover that Jesus is all we could hope him to be and more. And there are few ministry joys like when a Muslim friend gives their life to the Messiah. Plus, there are the bonuses of rich cross-cultural experience and amazing foods along the way! All ministry is hard in its own ways, this one included. But as you engage Muslims you will discover that this is a ministry of joy.

In the coming chapters we will learn to follow the example of our leader with the Samaritan woman at the well. By his grace may we see similar fruitfulness with Muslims:

> *Many of the Samaritans from that town believed in him because of the woman's testimony, "He told me everything I ever did." So when the Samaritans came to him, they urged him to stay with them, and he stayed two days. And because of his words many more became believers. They said to the woman, "We no longer believe just because of what you said; now we have heard for ourselves, and we know that this man really is the Savior of the world."*
>
> *John 4:39-42*

KEY POINTS

- In order to pursue a better future, face the messy history Christians and Muslims share (chapter 2).
- To minister with deeper awareness, recognize power dynamics between us and learn about Muslim identity (chapter 3).
- Stretch yourself to go out of your comfort zone and build gospel friendships with Muslims (chapter 4).
- Islam has both similarities to and differences from Christianity, but you can help Muslim friends meet Jesus personally in the pages of the Bible (chapter 5).
- Conversion is a process, and it is in good discipling that all new believers can grow to fuller understanding and maturity (chapters 6 and 7).
- The ultimate goal of international student ministry is that students who meet Christ while abroad will return as witnesses to their own families and communities (chapter 8).
- Ministry among Muslims will refresh you through inviting spiritual conversations, will deepen your faith as you wrestle for truth together, and will fill you with joy!

ACTION STEP

Re-read John 4:1-42 and journal about the parts of Jesus' interaction with the woman that move you. Pray, asking God to help you minister like Jesus.

PRAYER

Lord, thank you for the example you set of sensitive, courageous witness. I want to follow in your footsteps. As I read, give me the openness to learn difficult history and face cultural differences. Lead me out of my comfort zone to meet Muslims on their turf. Guide me into friendships where I can care for people and testify to your goodness in my life. Help me be faithful in my part of your story with Muslims, however small or large. And may I and those I serve experience the joy that this Samaritan woman found in you! Amen.

2 ACKNOWLEDGING MUSLIM-CHRISTIAN HISTORY

Those who do not learn history are doomed to repeat it.
- George Santayana

The past is never dead. It's not even past.
- William Faulkner

When you engage with a Muslim, you join a 1,400-year story of our faiths meeting. This chapter surveys five key eras from that history: the beginning of Islam, Christians living in the Islamic empire, the Crusades, the era of colonialism, and the 20th century. Along the way we will see wrongs committed by Christians but also encouraging moments of Christlike witness.

In the West, we tend to emphasize individualism over community. Many think, "I am responsible for my actions and my actions alone." This leads to treating history as things done by other people long ago and unrelated to my life choices. But hopefully you realize that though you are an individual, you are also connected to your family, your religion, your nation, and each of these groups' histories. They are part of how you understand yourself, and how others receive you.

Most Muslim international students come from communal cultures deeply connected to their history. They look to the past as an interpretive grid for understanding the present. This extends to how they relate to Christians. They have heard, more often than we, the stories of Christians under Muslim rule, Muslims under Christian rule, and dialogues and wars between our faiths. Those perceptions color our conversations together, and they influence a Muslim's ideas of what our faith is about.

We do not need an encyclopedic knowledge of history to start connecting with Muslims. But part of maturing is learning the back story and responding appropriately. Where Christians have misrepresented Jesus by regarding Muslims not as fellow people for whom Jesus' blood was shed, but as political or ideological enemies, cheap labor, or terrorists, we must repent. And where there are positive examples of Christians who engaged Muslims well, balancing sensitive respect with winsome courage, we can follow their examples on campus today.

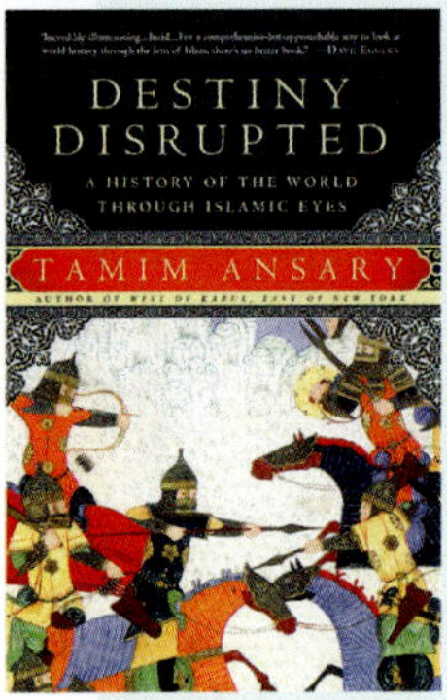

Have you ever wondered how your Muslim friends see their history? Afghan-American Tamim Ansary's *Destiny Disrupted: A History of the World Through Islamic Eyes* provides just that perspective. Ansary tells the story of Islam as a cultural insider, in prose that is like sitting on the porch with your grandfather listening to his favorite stories—if your grandfather were a learned scholar. He says, "My aim is mainly to convey what Muslims think happened, because that's what has motivated Muslims over the ages and what makes their role in world history intelligible."[4]

▶ 1. THE BEGINNING OF ISLAM

THE ORIGIN STORY

Scholars have had a notoriously difficult time studying the origins of Islam. The earliest Islamic account available today was written two centuries after Muhammad's death. And neither Muhammad, Mecca, nor Islam are mentioned in any non-Islamic works of the time, either. This does not mean the commonly told story is untrue. But it is important to note that what we know comes from sources within the religion, several hundred years after the events they depict, and after the Islamic community had grown into a

powerful empire.[5] Regardless of historical certainty, it is important to be familiar with the origin story because it is what Muslims believe. This is what your friends hold dear as *their* story.

According to Islamic sources, around the year 610 AD a young businessman named Muhammad from the city of Mecca, in present day Saudi Arabia, began to receive revelations from God through the angel *Jibril* (Gabriel). Muhammad may have been illiterate,[6] but as he spoke these revelations, a small band of followers began to form.

The story he conveyed was about the one true God whom all humans must believe in and obey. A judgment day would come when there would be a strong punishment for all who did not turn away from polytheism. This was a bold message in Mecca since the city's economy was built on idol worship, and in 622 AD Muhammad and his followers were driven out. They were welcomed in Medina, some 200 miles north.

The migration from Mecca to Medina, known as the *Hijra*, became a defining moment in the birth of Islam. As Muhammad's leadership and prestige grew, the revelations began to include detailed communal and political guidelines. Most Muslims today agree that the proper practice of Islam requires that the entire system--from family life to society to government—is aligned with Islamic teachings. There is no sacred/secular divide. Eventually, in 630 AD, Muhammad returned to conquer the city of Mecca and firmly established Islamic monotheism in the region.

Most Muslims today agree that the proper practice of Islam requires that the entire system–from family life to society to government–be aligned with Islamic teachings.

MUHAMMAD'S VIEW OF CHRISTIANS

By the year of the Hijra, Christianity was six hundred years old and firmly established from Asia to the Mediterranean, including on the Arabian Peninsula, according to historian Vince Bantu.[7] It is thus highly likely that Muhammad interacted with Christians. Indeed, the Qur'an frequently mentions Jesus, prior revelations from God, and Jews and Christians.

What is less clear is if Muhammad heard accurate Christian theology from those he met. At the time there was no Bible in the Arabic language, so stories would have been transmitted orally. Sura ("chapter" in the Qur'an) 5:116 says, "Allah said, 'Isa son of Mariam, did you tell the people: Take me and my mother as two gods in addition to Allah?'"[8] Christian readers will answer emphatically "No!" The sura appears to be based on a misunderstanding of the Trinity. In this and other places, the Qur'an seems to describe (or reject) beliefs that are not actually part of Christianity.

Muhammad initially appeared willing to connect his calling to Judaism and Christianity. Sura 2:89 describes the revelation given as a confirmation of the previous holy books, which were the Torah and the Gospel.[9] The Qur'an refers to Jews and Christians as "people of the book." Sura 5:68 challenges the people of the book, saying that "[you] have no foundation unless you uphold the *Tawrat* (Torah) and *Injil* (Gospel) and what was revealed to you by your Lord." Verses like these[10] open up interesting conversation paths with Muslims.

But elsewhere the Qur'an strikes a more hostile tone and portrays Islam as a corrective. Sura 9:30 calls Christians liars who oppose Allah. How should we interpret the discrepancy? Most scholars separate suras into "Meccan" (earlier) and "Medinan" (later) revelations. According to this view, Muhammad may have originally hoped to be accepted as a prophet by Jews and Christians. When he was not--and as his own influence grew--his posture toward them changed. Many Muslims use the Meccan and Medinan labels, but these titles are not actually part of the Qur'an.[11]

ISLAM'S EARLY EXPANSION

Muhammad died in 632 AD, causing a crisis in the Islamic community: who should succeed him as the next leader? This is how the split between Shi'a and Sunni Islam began, which continues to today.[12] The first four *caliphs*, or leaders, faced internal conflicts and rivalries. But the Muslim armies were effective at conquering neighboring lands, including many Christian-majority regions. By the eighth century the Islamic empire stretched from Andalusia (modern Spain) to the Indus River in modern-day Pakistan. A mere century after it was born, Islam had reshaped a large portion of the world and become a global religion.

Christians connecting with Muslims today need to be familiar with the beginnings of Islam. First, remember that the story comes to us only from Islamic accounts, unlike Christ and the early church which are mentioned by multiple non-Christian historians of the time. Yet the origin narrative is precious to our friends, so we should tread carefully. Second, understand that many parts of the Qur'an paint a portrait of continuation from Christianity, though with some problematic theology. We will return to this point in more detail in chapter 5, with ideas for conversation and reading scripture with your friends.

▶ 2. CHRISTIANS IN THE ISLAMIC EMPIRE

We hear a fair amount today about religious freedom–-how Christians fare in Islamic countries. But what was it like through history? By 750 AD, due to rapid military conquest, the Islamic Abbasid dynasty ruled over perhaps half of the world's Christians.[13]

In the caliphate, Christians were *dhimmi*, a status for minority groups. Though this meant certain protections, it also put restrictions on faith practices. Christians were required to pay a special tax, and at times church buildings were destroyed. Believers could not speak against Muhammad nor proselytize Muslims, nor could they prevent other Christians from converting to Islam. Still, many well-educated Christians held influential positions in

SPREAD OF ISLAM 610 – 1258 AD

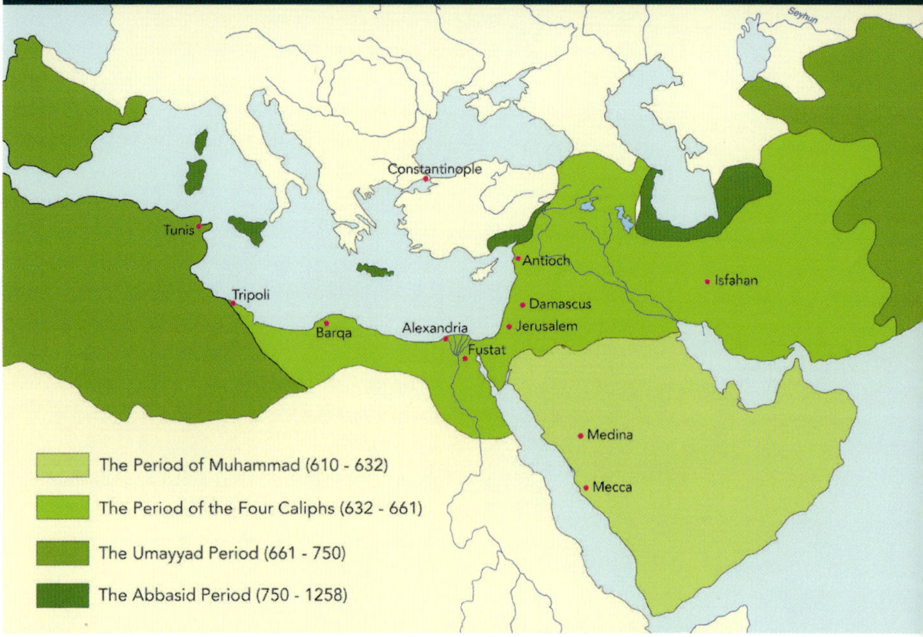

society as doctors, academics, teachers, and book translators. They were involved in important projects and served among the Islamic elite.[14]

Despite the restrictions on them, some Christians in the caliphate exercised truly faithful and creative witness. As locals, they understood their neighbors well and could connect with Muslim minds and hearts. Names like Abu Ra'ita, Abu Qurra, and Ammar al-Basri are unknown in the West, but these scholar-theologian Christians were brilliant witnesses who dug deep into Islam to present Jesus in ways that Muslims could relate to. They wrote in Arabic,[15] argued from the Qur'an itself, adopted Islamic idioms, and even entered Muslims' own internal theological discussions in order to draw analogies to the Trinity.[16]

> *Christians in the caliphate entered into a Muslim framework of thought to show the validity of a Christian view of Christ in terms that Muslims might understand as credible.*[17]
>
> *- Mark Beaumont*

Living under Islamic rule also meant that Christian witnesses learned to be discerning with their words. Patriarch Timothy of Baghdad oversaw a network of churches over several million square miles from Turkey to China. In 781 AD, the patriarch had a peaceful dialogue with Caliph al-

Mahdi in which he answered questions and reasoned for Christian faith. When asked about Muhammad, Timothy said that he "walked in the path of the prophets" and affirmed positives, like turning the people from polytheism, but stopped short of calling Muhammad an actual prophet. And the Patriarch never criticized the Qur'an itself, but rather Muslim interpretations of it.[18]

Today it seems that Muslims and Christians often choose *either* arguing for our faith *or* working together. Yet from one thousand years ago, we have powerful examples of both happening at the same time. People lived and worked together while also passionately discussing theological differences. One contemporary opportunity is for us to find common ground living in our secular culture. My Muslim friends share similar concerns to me about morality, family, and religious freedom. We have an opportunity to grow closer together addressing common challenges while still engaging the distinctives of our faiths.

▶ 3. THE CRUSADES

> *[The Crusades are] often relegated to a few pages in Western world-history books. For the Muslim, this violation is kept vibrantly alive through writings and oral traditions. Can the Christian humbly apologize for his ancestors' part in committing a "Christian jihad?"*[19]
>
> *- Phil Parshall*

OUR DARKEST HOUR

Unfortunately, the positive approaches to witness during the Abbasid dynasty would soon be eclipsed by one of the darkest periods in our shared history: the Crusades. A millennium later, the specter of these religious wars still hovers in the background when Muslims and Christians meet.

By the eleventh century, Muslims oversaw a vast empire including much of the Holy Land. In 1096, Pope Urban II called on Christians to retake Jerusalem. Many responded enthusiastically, raising their own funds and traveling up to thousands of miles to participate.

The Crusaders took Antioch and then Jerusalem. There the European armies, with the cross of Christ emblazoned on their shields, committed unspeakable atrocities. They massacred Muslim inhabitants and burned down a synagogue full of Jews seeking refuge. Reading how these acts of violence were justified with spiritual language is stomach-churning. Over the following two centuries there were many more crusades, with similar brutalities and massive loss of life on all sides.

"...a general slaughter of the pagans took place. No one was spared... one inescapable death awaited them all. ...They approached the sepulchre of the Lord and thanked Him for what they had sought, the liberation of the Blessed Places; He had performed such great deeds with them as his instruments."[20]

- The Deeds of God Through the Franks, Guibert of Nogent

Taking of Jerusalem by the Crusaders, Émile Signol

What made Christians so willing to take up arms? Irvin and Sunquist describe a variety of motivations.[21] Spiritual reasons were prominent, such as participating in a "holy" war or pilgrimage, which were believed by some to grant forgiveness of sin. Seeking justice was a reason, as many crusaders saw themselves as liberating Christians from oppressive Muslim rule. Fear was another motivator, as the Islamic military continued to advance into Christian territory. There were also material reasons, as some crusaders went seeking bounty and land from their conquests.

...the Arabic term used for 'Crusader,' Salibi, *literally 'Crosser' or one who bears the cross, serves to reinforce the already well-established Muslim suspicion of the symbol of the Cross..."*[22]

- Hugh Goddard

PEACEFUL WITNESS IN A TIME OF VIOLENCE

In the midst of this chaos, we find an account of truly Christlike witness by Francis of Assisi. The peacemaking friar made multiple attempts to cross into Islamic territory in order to argue the error of the crusaders' ways and to share Christ with Muslims. Each attempt put his own life at serious risk.

Francis of Assisi before Sultan al-Kamil of Egypt, unknown painter

Francis finally succeeded in 1219 and was received in the court by Sultan al-Kamil of Egypt. Accounts of their encounter vary, but it seems each testified to the other and afterward Francis was sent away with a gift of goodwill.[23] Like Francis, when we speak of Jesus we must resemble Jesus, who clothed himself in weakness (Philippians 2) and broke down dividing walls of hostility (Ephesians 2).

The Crusades are a humbling reminder that we Christians have been on the wrong side of history at times. It is right to name contemporary injustices and oppression done by Muslims, such as 9/11, Boko Haram's and the Taliban's abuse of women, and the deeds of ISIS. But it is also right to call out Christians when our own faith family sins against others.

▶ 4. THE ERA OF COLONIALISM

BRINGING THE BIBLE, CULTURE, AND CHAINS

Between the 15th and 19th centuries, European nations exploring new territory colonized many Muslim-majority lands. The Christian colonial powers oppressed people while sharing a gospel wrapped in European culture. They forced their government, education, and clothing styles on the colonized, believing, as Hanciles commented, "real Christians looked and behaved like Europeans."[24] Local populations were denigrated and often enslaved.

Most of today's Muslim world was affected by colonization. Britain occupied parts of modern Egypt, India, Pakistan, and Bangladesh plus Afghanistan and parts of the Arabian Peninsula. Portugal colonized parts

Bali, Indonesia

of west Africa, while France had colonies across west, central, and north Africa. Spain colonized the Philippines, and the Dutch colonized Indonesia. Moving geographically away from the European powers, Russia was involved in Central Asia.[25] Every one of these places has its own stories that need to be heard, particularly by the sensitive Christian befriending Muslims from there.

Colonization is a complex topic. There is no denying that it was a means by which the gospel reached new audiences. As such, some say it actually accelerated Christianity taking on a more global identity.[26] And some Muslims are thankful for the Western medicine and culture that foreign powers brought to their countries.

But when Christian witness follows the pattern of worldly politics—cultural superiority, conquest, and subjugation—there are consequences. Today Christianity has a legacy of oppression in many places, and Muslims around the world see it as unmistakably foreign, a Western export with no place in their culture. This naturally colors how they respond to the gospel, and how converts are perceived by their communities.[27]

Some Christians today avoid sharing their faith at all out of fear of imposing culture and "colonizing" others. But silence is not the antidote to colonization. Jesus commanded us to make disciples of all nations (Matthew 28). We must do so, with gentleness and respect (I Peter 3), while making every effort to honor our Muslim friends' cultures. In the coming chapters we will discuss ways to do this.

AN INDIGENOUS CHURCH

There were, however, local believers who sought to contextualize biblical faith for their own people. Indonesian historian Sutarman Pardonati[28] wrote about Sadrach Surapranata (1835-1924), who was a devout Javanese

Muslim until becoming a follower of Jesus in his thirties. The Dutch Reformed Church, the predominant foreign Christian influence in Indonesia at the time, was particularly harsh to the locals. They viewed Indonesians as ethnically inferior and, unsurprisingly, the Muslims had a low view in return–calling the Dutch church "the religion of pig manure."[29]

Sadrach set out to develop a church model that fit his Javanese people while staying within biblical boundaries, as Parshall explained. These believers called themselves Christians and their church building a mosque. They continued to wear Javanese clothing. Believers sat on the floor with women and men separated. They recited a modified version of the *shahada*, or declaration of faith, alongside the Apostle's Creed. The church used the terms *Isa* (Jesus) and *Allah* (God) but did not affirm Muhammad as a prophet.[30]

In contrast to the Dutch Calvinists who nearly abandoned their mission due to low responsiveness, Sadrach's movement grew to 7,500 believers with Muslim backgrounds.[31] The missionaries accused it of being a sinful Islamic sect and attempted, unsuccessfully, to suppress it. After Sadrach's death, the community dissolved and its lasting impact is unclear.[32] Yet this is the first known large-scale movement to Christ among Muslims.

▶ 5. UPHEAVAL IN THE 20TH-21ST CENTURIES

Tamim Ansary asserts that in recent centuries Muslims "feel that something had gone awry with the flow" of history. This is the disrupted destiny his book title describes.[33] In their eyes, Muhammad birthed a pure faith community, and rapid expansion during the first centuries was evidence of God's blessing. But then the caliphate slid into stagnation, and colonial powers moved in and subjugated Muslims. And in the 20th century, Muslim identity and solidarity has been still further challenged by both international affairs and internal conflicts.

No discussion of Muslim-Christian history can overlook the modern state of Israel, founded in 1948 following the horrors of the Holocaust. For nine hundred years Muslims held the Holy Land, which is venerated in Islam as in Judaism and Christianity. When Western powers agreed to relocate Jews to Palestine, Zionists—and many American and British Christian supporters—celebrated it as "a land without a people for a people without a land." Seven hundred thousand Palestinians who were forcefully relocated from their homeland saw the situation differently, as do Muslims around the world today. To them Israel represents one more chapter in Western aggression.

The Dome of the Rock on the Temple Mount in Jerusalem, a city revered in Judaism, Christianity, and Islam

Few would disagree that Jews needed a safe home, but Christians disagree about the spiritual significance of the modern state of Israel.[34] As we seek to be Christlike witnesses among Muslims, we must be deeply sensitive to our friends' perspectives on occupation, refugees, settlement building, the separation wall, and land rights issues in Israel/Palestine.

Efforts at Islamic unity have generally been unsuccessful in the past century. Both Pan-Arabism (political renewal) and the Muslim Brotherhood (religious renewal) have largely failed to bring the Middle East and North Africa (MENA) together. Sunni/Shi'a divides are as deep as ever. Sunni Saudi Arabia and Shi'a Iran invest massive amounts of money to spread their influence to other Muslim contexts. Their proxy war in Yemen has killed nearly a quarter million other Muslims and created a colossal humanitarian crisis.[35] The Arab Spring in 2011 offered a brief hope of justice and societal renewal, but that spark was snuffed out within just a few years, disillusioning thousands of Muslim youth.

Wars during the past century between Muslim-majority countries and other nations are frequently viewed through the lens of crusade, the latest chapters of Islam versus Christianity. After Afghanistan prevailed over the Soviet Union in the 1980s, some of those *mujahideen*, Islamic fighters, traveled to Bosnia & Herzegovina to fight alongside Muslims there against Catholic Croats and Orthodox Serbs. And many Muslims see the Global War on Terrorism since 9/11, which includes the War in Afghanistan (2001 - 2021) and Iraq War (2003 - 2011) as Western Christian imperialism.

> *Too many Westerners take refuge in simplistic explanations: fanaticism, extremism, "fundamentalism," insanity. Such dismissals advance the task of comprehension not one jot...They indicate not so much an understanding as a refusal to understand.*[36]
>
> *– Meic Pearse*

Westerners are often profoundly unaware of how our countries' decisions have unexpected consequences. The media portrays Iran as a rogue state, but how many know our own countries' role in contributing to it? In 1953 Western intelligence agents helped oust Iran's elected leader to return the pro-West shah, who unfortunately was known for brutality.[37] Twenty-six years later the Islamic Revolution happened, bringing an oppressively fundamentalist government to power over a mostly nominal Persian Muslim population.

CONCLUSION: THE PATH FORWARD

> **An InterVarsity campus minister related the following story**: "Once a Christian friend and I were talking with a Muslim woman who began to get visibly upset describing how the policies of the United States, my country, affected her people. My friend started to cry and apologized for the actions that were damaging to Muslims and misrepresented our faith. It took me off guard and had an even deeper effect on the Muslim woman. She also broke down in tears and threw her arms around my friend in an embrace. There was a lot of healing in that moment, simply because a Christian asked for forgiveness."

I am passionate about sharing the gospel with everyone in my life, and since you are reading this, I trust you are, too. One of my greatest fears is that my own flaws will get in the way of the message of Jesus and people will be unable to "taste and see that the Lord is good" (Psalm 34:8).

Sadly, the sins of our ancestors *have* at times blocked Muslims from experiencing Jesus. Let us not presume that we would have done better in their place. Instead, let us engage in corporate repentance, like Nehemiah did on behalf of his ancestors (Nehemiah 1), and pledge ourselves to a better path forward. Like in the story above, asking forgiveness is powerful.

There are also positive historical examples of Christians connecting with Muslims with grace and truth. We celebrate them, and we know there are countless more from the past 1,400 years, far from the headlines. You, too, are playing your part. Picking up a newly arrived Muslim international student from the airport, sharing a meal and good conversation, telling stories from Jesus' life and ministry, offering prayer... all of these contribute to the story God is writing. It is to these tasks—the many things we can do to represent Christ well among Muslims today—that we now turn.

KEY POINTS

- When we connect with Muslims today, we join a long history of Christian-Muslim engagement which our Muslim friends are already familiar with.
- Many parts of the Qur'an, believed to be the earliest, paint Islam as a continuation of Judaism and Christianity and affirm our holy books. Other parts take a more confrontational tone.
- Christians living under the Islamic empire faced significant restrictions, yet they also witnessed with courage and insight.
- The Crusades were a tragic chapter of history that still hovers in the background when Christians and Muslims meet today.
- During the era of colonization, outsiders mixed faith and culture unhelpfully which caused Muslims to see the gospel as a foreign idea. This idea persists today.
- In the past century the Islamic world has faced serious upheaval, related to both the actions of Muslim-majority nations and the actions of Western nations.

ACTION STEP

Read Nehemiah 1 for an example of corporate repentance, which is seeking God's forgiveness on behalf of sins committed by an entire community. Note how Nehemiah owns wrongs done as if they are his own and also prays with boldness for God to guide him forward.

PRAYER

Sovereign Lord, we repent of the sins of Christians through history toward Muslims: of violence and wars, muddling the gospel by adding our culture and politics, and treating Muslims as enemies rather than people you created, love, and whom Jesus died for. You have shown us what is good and what you require of us: to do justice, to love mercy, and to walk humbly before You. Move us into action pursuing justice, responding both to the spiritual and social needs of Muslims. Make us merciful toward those who have sinned against us and other Christians through the centuries. And help us walk humbly before you in our engagement with Muslims today. May your kingdom come, Amen.

3 UNDERSTANDING MUSLIM INTERNATIONAL STUDENTS

At an international student retreat a few years ago I marveled at the variety of Muslim attendees. Shafiq came to the group sessions on edge, ready to argue for Islam at the drop of a hat. Faisal avoided serious conversations and slipped away at every opportunity to smoke hookah with anyone who would join him. Noor painted henna on the hands of five other women and laughed off the non-Muslim boys who didn't know better and asked for their own henna tattoos. Ali strummed his oud, a traditional mandolin-like instrument. And everyone enjoyed canoeing, paintball, and taking selfies.

It would be a mistake to approach this chapter with the assumption that all Muslims are the same. Of course they are not. They are Sunni and Shi'a, Indonesian and Bahraini and Iranian. They are male and female, conservative and liberal, devout and nominal. This isn't surprising given that Islam is the second largest religion in the world. It is important to avoid generalizations and thinking that because you know one Muslim, you understand them all. We must treat each person uniquely, just as we want to be treated.

On the other hand, there *are* commonalities across the world's Muslims. In this chapter we will outline the main beliefs and practices of Islam, and then consider some of the elements of Muslim identity that you are sure to encounter. Understanding these will help you relate well with your friends.

ISLAM'S SIX CORE BELIEFS

> *Righteousness is believing in Allah, the last day, the angels, the book and the prophets, giving money in his love to relatives, orphans, the poor, travelers, and beggars, freeing slaves, performing prayers, paying the poor-tax, keeping their promises, and enduring misery and adversity.*
>
> *Qur'an 2:177*

A person who follows Islam is a Muslim. "Islam" simply means submission. "Muslim" means "one who submits to the will of God." Islam has six core beliefs and five practices known as the "Five Pillars of Islam." As you read about each, consider the similarities and differences from Christianity and your own faith practices.

BELIEF THAT GOD IS ONE

The "oneness" of God, *tawhid*, is central to Muslim understanding and is affirmed multiple times a day during prayer. Islam forbids associating God with anything else. He is utterly, wholly different from creation. Christians are often accused of being polytheists because of belief in the Trinity, which is considered an attack on God's oneness and transcendence. Christians also believe in God's transcendence ("No one is like you, Lord," Jeremiah 10:6) but that it is coupled with voluntary immanence: God chose to take on human form and enter his creation (Philippians 2).

BELIEF IN ANGELS

Muslims believe that God's angels exist to serve him and do his will, including delivering messages. The angel *Jibril* (Gabriel) visited Muhammad throughout his life, delivering the revelation of the Qur'an piece by piece. Christians also regard angels as messengers of God's will (Hebrews 1:7,14). In the Bible, Gabriel is the primary messenger of God.

BELIEF IN HOLY BOOKS

Islam teaches that God has given humankind four books for guidance: the *Tawrat, Zabur, Injil* and Qur'an. The first three correspond, respectively, to the Bible's Torah (also known as the Pentateuch, the first five books of the Old Testament), the Psalms and wisdom literature, and the Gospel message. Christians will be pleasantly surprised to learn that Muslims esteem a large part of our Bible. However, most Muslims have been told

that the original *Tawrat, Zabur* and *Injil* have been corrupted[38] or lost to history and only the Qur'an is valid today. For this reason, the majority have never read the other books. It is commonly taught that there is no need to, as the Qur'an holds all that is important for a godly life.

Muslims believe the Qur'an is the exact words of God, handed down in the Arabic language. Translated versions are therefore not the actual Qur'an,[39] so Muslims learn to recite the text in Arabic, even though 80% or more of the world's Muslims do not speak the language.[40] In contrast, Christians believe that Jesus is the living Word of God and affirm Bible translations (not just the original Hebrew and Greek) that accurately communicate the message of Jesus. A shorthand, if imperfect, way of remembering this is to say that the Qur'an is to Muslims what Jesus is to Christians.

In addition to the Qur'an, Muslims are guided by *hadith*, massive collections of texts containing stories from Muhammad's life. These are believed to have been faithfully transferred from one hearer to the next until they were written down, though their historicity is difficult to verify. Shi'as and Sunnis disagree about *hadith*.

BELIEF IN PROPHETS

According to Islam, throughout history God has sent prophets to deliver his message so that no generation is without excuse. Twenty-five prophets are recognized in Islam, though some lesser *hadith* hint that there may have been more than 100,000. Each taught the same monotheistic message.

The best-known prophets correspond to biblical figures: Adam (Adam), Nuh (Noah), Ibrahim (Abraham), Musa (Moses), Dawud (David), Yahya (John the Baptist), and Isa (Jesus). Muhammad is considered the final prophet of Islam, whose message is the standard by which to evaluate all others.

COMMON PROPHETS (SEE APPENDIX D)

ISLAM	CHRISTIANITY
Adam	Adam (Genesis 2-5)
Nuh	Noah (Genesis 5-9)
Ibrahim	Abram/Abraham (Genesis 11-25)
Yusuf	Joseph (Genesis 30-50)
Musa	Moses (Exodus 2 - Deuteronomy 34)
Dawud	David (1 Samuel 16 - 1 Kings 2)
Sulaiman	Solomon (1 Kings 1-11)
Ilias	Elijah (1 Kings 17 - 2 Kings 2)
Al-Yasa	Elisha (1 Kings 19 - 2 Kings 13)
Ayub	Job (Job 1-42)
Yunus	Jonah (Jonah 1-4)
Yahya	John the Baptist (Mark 1-6)
Isa	Jesus (Matthew 1 - Acts 1)

BELIEF IN A DAY OF JUDGMENT

Muslims believe that God will judge all humankind with either the reward of paradise or the punishment of hell. The Qur'an describes the way to be saved in a variety of ways, including a combination of faith and good deeds (Q 3:133-136), God's sovereignty (Q 4:47-48, 5:18), avoiding major sins (Q 4:31), God's mercy (Q 39:53), and good deeds taking away evil deeds (Q 11:114).

Most ordinary Muslims say that if they seek to do good and practice the Five Pillars (below) they can *hope* to reach paradise. They will not, however, speak with certainty. Unlike Christianity, which bases the hope of salvation on Christ's finished work on the cross, in Islam God's decision awaits the judgment day. Then he will weigh each person's good and bad deeds. Therefore, it would be presumptive to assert the outcome.[41]

BELIEF IN GOD'S WILL

In Islam, God is the cause of every event that occurs, and humans must submit to his will in all aspects of life. Muslims acknowledge this by often adding the Arabic term *inshallah*, "If God wills it," when making plans. The emphasis on God's decree is so strong that at times it sounds like fatalism. But Islam also teaches human responsibility for our choices, which puts Muslims in a similar position to Christians as they attempt to explain the paradox of free will and sovereignty. Interestingly, despite believing in divine determinism, many Muslims around the world spend much time and money on rituals to influence their destiny (see "Fear and Power," below).

ISLAM'S FIVE PILLARS, OR CENTRAL PRACTICES

> *Islam has been built on five [pillars]: testifying that there is no god but Allah and that Muhammad is the Messenger of Allah, performing the prayers, paying the alms, making the pilgrimage to the House, and fasting in Ramadan.*
>
> *- Sahih Muslim Book 1, Hadith 1*

These five central practices[42] make up the heart of Muslim spirituality.

SHAHADA, THE STATEMENT OF FAITH

To become a Muslim, one simply recites the statement "There is no god but God, and Muhammad is the prophet of God" with genuine belief. This declaration, or *shahada*, is at the heart of Islam. It is recited in Arabic by Muslims around the world in formal prayers five times per day, which involves repeating the shahada as many as seventeen times in total. Many also recite it spontaneously for spiritual protection and reassurance.

SALAT, PRAYER

"Prayer is the high point of Muslim worship," an *imam*, a leader of a mosque, once told me. Muslims are commanded to pray five times per day, in the mosque if possible. Islamic prayer is scripted and involves standing, kneeling and prostrating in lines with others, with women and men separate. Muslims are proud of the bond of communal prayer, and the image of hundreds or thousands praying in rows during Ramadan is moving indeed. Though it is not forbidden, it is unlikely that your Muslim friends practice spontaneous or intercessory prayer.

ZAKAT, ALMS

Islam regulates that all Muslims give 2.5% of the value of all their possessions away annually to the poor and needy. In some nations the contribution is voluntary, while other Muslim-majority countries mandate *zakat*.

SAWM, FASTING

During Ramadan, the ninth month of the lunar Islamic calendar, Muslims fast from food and water, drink, smoking, and sexual intercourse from sunrise to sunset. This spiritual practice becomes grueling when Ramadan falls

Breaking the Ramadan fast after sunset

during the summer, with extreme heat and long days! Muslims fast for self-restraint (Q 2:183) and also to gain merit and forgiveness of sins (Q 33:35).

HAJJ, PILGRIMAGE

At least once in their lifetime all Muslims who are able are expected to go on pilgrimage to Mecca, Saudi Arabia. There, over six days, they will pray with fellow Muslims in The Prophet's Mosque, walk in circles around the *Ka'aba* (a sacred stone), repent of their sins, and throw stones at a pillar symbolizing the devil. Going on *hajj* is considered a supreme honor. Once a Muslim has been they may change something about their clothing or adopt the title "*Hajj*" as a testament to the experience.

▶ DYNAMICS OF MUSLIM CULTURES

If we were covering only the traditional view of religion, the chapter would end here having addressed formal Islamic beliefs. But a deeper understanding, sometimes called the anthropological view of religion, includes all the traditions and values of a people group–-how they navigate life. How an international student understands "being Muslim" comes not just from theological doctrines but from their background and lived experience.

The main Muslim world regions,[43] all of which send international students to the West, are the Middle East/North Africa (MENA), South Asia, Southeast Asia, Sub-Saharan Africa, and Central Asia.[44] The following cultural elements are important to know as you build relationships with internationals from every region.

You may find yourself relating to some of these dynamics from your own culture. If so, you are blessed to have an area of commonality to explore in conversation with Muslims. And if you are not familiar with these, adhering to the suggestions given may help you avoid blunders that could trigger an international crisis. Kidding! Mostly.

IDENTITY AND PRACTICE

> *"But I am Muslim... If I began believing in God, I must choose Islam! It is our religion."*

This is what an atheist international once told me, while we were having a conversation about Jesus. Though this student did not even have faith, he still identified personally as part of the Muslim community.

I have heard many outsiders categorize a woman who does not cover her head or a man who seldom visits the mosque, as nominal or "not *really* Muslim." Not only is this judgment crudely inappropriate, it is too simplistic. Muslim identity is multifaceted. Spiritual practices like praying, reading the Qur'an, fasting, and wearing the hijab are some indicators of that identity, but not the entirety of it. In Malaysia, "Muslim" is a defined ethnic group. Regardless of their personal beliefs, ethnic Malays are classified Muslims on government IDs. In Bosnia and Herzegovina, going through war and ethnic cleansing as a community instilled a deep connection to "being Muslim" even in very nominal Muslims.

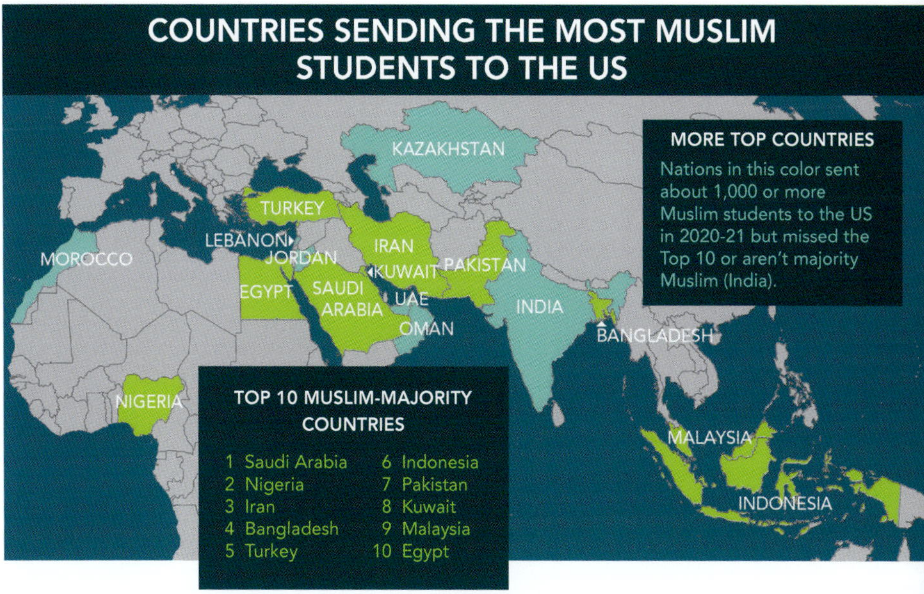

It is helpful to think of identity and practice as two axes of a graph. Consider four hypothetical Muslims:

PRACTICE
Islamic rituals and spiritual practices

IDENTITY
Connection to "being Muslim"

HIGHER PRACTICE / LOWER PRACTICE

LOWER IDENTITY / HIGHER IDENTITY

IV. High Practice, Low Identity

AISHA prays daily, wears a "Hand of Fatima" necklace—to ward off curses, or possibly just as jewelry—and speaks freely about spirituality and God's love. She believes all religions teach basically the same message of doing good. Some of her friends say she sounds "new-agey." In her African home country Aisha read literature from *sufis*, or Muslim mystics. Aisha is a high practice, low identity Muslim.

I. High Practice, High Identity

RASUL comes from a devout Arab family. He prays five times a day, either at the mosque or in his dorm room, and knows a *hadith* for every life situation. Rasul feels deeply connected to the *Umma*, or global Islamic community. He enjoys the company of Christians he has met in the US and accepts any opportunity to explain the superiority of his faith, supplemented by YouTube apologetics videos. He is a high practice, high identity Muslim.

III. Low Practice, Low Identity

ALI is an Iranian PhD student studying physics. His parents became disillusioned and abandoned faith in response to the harsh version of Islam they experienced in their country. Ali has never cared much about religion. He is proud of the rich poetic and intellectual tradition in his Persian culture and deep-down feels that religious leaders stifled it—though he is cautious about speaking such things openly. Ali is glad to be in the West and eager to try new things while studying here. He is a low identity, low practice Muslim.

II. Low Practice, High Identity

FATIMA loves the food and traditions of her Southeast Asian culture. She doesn't know much of the Qur'an since she cannot read Arabic, but she celebrates every holiday and wears a hijab as is expected of a respectful young woman. Her parents are currently making a marriage match for her with a young man also studying in the States. Though she does not talk about spirituality much, she feels safe and accepted in community with other Muslims. She is a low practice, high identity Muslim.

Each of these international students is Muslim but lives it out differently. And although we named locations, diversity exists within each of those locations (i.e., Ali may be low identity/low practice while his brother is deeply devout).

SUNNI AND SHI'A

> *Just as John the Baptist prepared the way for Jesus, Ayatollah Khomeini prepared our people for Jesus.*
>
> *- An Iranian follower of Christ*

The world's Muslims are divided into two main theological groups: Sunni and Shi'a. This distinction is one of the most significant among Muslim international students. The vast majority (85%) of the Islamic world is Sunni.[45] Shi'as are predominant in Iran and also make up a significant population in Iraq, India, Pakistan, Turkey, Yemen, and eastern Saudi Arabia.

The schism between Sunni and Shi'a began immediately after Muhammad's death in a conflict about who should succeed him as leader. The group who became Shi'as backed the loser and has been oppressed and the minority through most of history. Each year on the holiday *Ashura*, Shi'as commemorate the martyrdom of Husayn, Muhammad's grandson. They believe God has sent a series of *mahdis*, messiahs, through

Shi'a women mourn during Ashura ceremonies in Turkey

history and await a future *mahdi* who will bring peace and justice and be accompanied by Jesus.[46] Ask your Shi'a friends about these beliefs and explore the connections to the Christian understanding of Jesus' atonement and second coming.

God is working powerfully among Shi'a Muslims. Iran is believed to have the fastest growing movement to Christ in the world, growing from about 500 believers in the late 1980s to an estimated 500,000+ today.[47] Some of this can be attributed to the rigid Islamic fundamentalism and oppression by the Islamic Republic of Iran, which has turned many off to Islam. One Iranian student began reading the Bible secretly before coming to the US When he arrived, the first stop was a furniture giveaway by a ministry serving international students. He then went to coffee with the staff worker and asked all his questions about Jesus, the Bible and Christianity. That same day of his arrival, he began following Christ.

COMMUNAL > INDIVIDUALIST CULTURE

> *Islam is the whole warp and woof of society—in the family, in politics, in social relationships. To leave the Muslim faith is to break with one's society. Many a modern, educated Muslim is not all that religiously minded; but he must, nevertheless, remain a Muslim for social reasons, and also because it is the basis for his political belief. This makes it almost unthinkable for most Muslims even to consider the possibility of becoming a follower of some other religion.*[48]
>
> *- Martin Goldsmith*

At a student getaway in the mountains, a pastor was asked to explain the gospel to a group of twenty Muslims. He went off script and gave a "call to faith," inviting students to raise their hands and become Christians. No one did. As I looked around the room, I saw a number of the students exchanging perplexed looks with one another. One young woman later said, "I don't understand what he was asking. Did he want us to leave our families?"

In communal cultures, identity and meaning come through belonging to a group, and it is very important to make decisions that align with the community's expectations. This describes the majority of the world's peoples, including nearly all Muslims. An individualistic mindset, in contrast, emphasizes personal autonomy and independent decision making. This describes mainstream Western culture since the Enlightenment.

In communal cultures, identity and meaning come through belonging to a group, and it is important to make decisions that align with the community's expectations.

The opportunity to study in the West is a chance to pursue a career that will bring honor to Muslim internationals' extended family back home. But moving internationally is a deeply disorienting experience for communal people. Though some international students travel with spouses and children, far more arrive alone. Here, far from their community, they are offered more individual freedom and choices than ever before.

As the quote from Goldsmith above expresses, communal thinking deeply influences how Muslims feel about other religions. Many Westerners' testimonies include a moment when they could no longer follow what their parents believed and needed to investigate for themselves. For most Muslims, this moment simply does not exist. They certainly may have questions. But the thought of breaking free of the security and stability of one's family's tradition is deeply dissonant.

SHAME AND HONOR

> *Americans invite friends to your birthday celebration and then ask them to pay for themselves and you! In my country we take our friends out on our birthday and pay for them. It's a way of showing that we are honored by their friendship.*
>
> *- A Muslim international*

> *The West has a strong value for individual rights, but the Islamic world has a strong sense of duty to community.*
>
> *- Martin Accad*

On the day he prayed to trust Jesus, Adeel was ecstatic. He was eager to share the news with his family, and so with the encouraging prayers of his American friends he picked up the phone. "Dad and Mom, I've become a Christian," he said cautiously. After a lengthy pause that filled the air, his father gruffly responded, "You are no longer our son" and hung up.

Honor and shame are ways people experience moral rightness and wrongness, often described in contrast to innocence and guilt. Honor is bestowed through fulfilling group expectations and having good social standing.[49] A Muslim who goes to the west and becomes a successful doctor brings honor to her family back home--the neighbors will hear about it! Someone with a bad reputation carries shame and must seek restoration from his community or be removed from it, as Adeel experienced.

Every human culture in the world identifies with honor and shame, innocence and guilt, and power and fear (see next section) to differing degrees. These frameworks also describe how we "feel" our standing to be before God. In chapter 6 we will learn how to contextualize the gospel message according to these frameworks.

Honor/shame dynamics saturate our interactions with Muslims. Many Muslims would never question or disagree with an older professor or ministry volunteer. And if you ask your friend directly, "Will you come to our movie night?" receiving a "no" answer would shame you the inviter and so bring shame on your friend. Instead, she may say "yes" or "I would like that" and then not come. Instead, say "I'd love for you to come to our movie night if you are able." This indirect offer saves face by not forcing one person to disappoint the other.

FEAR AND POWER

> *While staying with some friends in the Middle East, I noticed that one woman's light was on all night. My host told me that this was because the woman, like many others, was afraid of the dark. "Jinn live in the dark and she is afraid she will be attacked while she sleeps, so she keeps her light on. It keeps the fear away."*

Tragically, many Muslims live in fear. There are many reasons. Physical abuse of women and children causes many to fear fathers and husbands. *Jinn*, demonic spirits in Islam, are believed to oppress people. Many Muslims fear dark spiritual power like curses. Physical abuse of women and children causes some to fear fathers and husbands. And on an existential level, the lack of certainty in salvation means Muslims fear failing to reach heaven. According to one *hadith*, Muhammad himself said, "By Allah, though I am Allah's Apostle, I neither know what will happen to me, nor to you."[50] Scary words, indeed.

Fear leads many Muslims to seek power and protection through popular, or folk, Islamic practices.[51] Some visit shamans or healers for help, or shrines seeking blessing. The Evil Eye and the Hand of Fatima, amulets to block curses, are two of the most commonly used power objects. The Qur'an itself may be treated as a mystical power object, especially among non-Arabic speaking Muslims. Learn more from your international

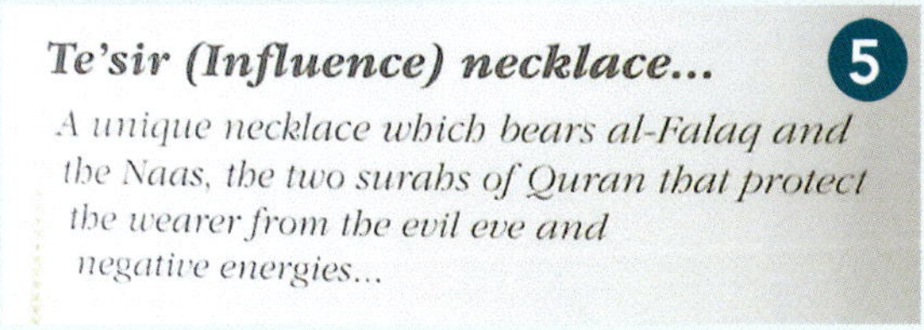

(1) The Evil Eye and the (2) Hand of Fatima are amulets Muslims around the world display to block curses and bring good fortune. They appear everywhere, including in (3) handmade gifts on Etsy or Amazon. Qur'anic verses are also used for protection, as illustrated by (4-5) this jewelry sold in Istanbul airport (ca.2015).

student friends by asking what people in their country do when someone is struggling with fear, recurring nightmares, or persistent bad luck, and other methods fail.

MEN AND WOMEN

> *I thought Hamza was enjoying our spiritual conversation, and then suddenly he asked me if I would be his girlfriend!*
>
> *- A Christian student*

In general, Muslim cultures are far more conservative about gender roles than in the West. There is little mixing of unmarried women and men in social settings, and virtually no touching. Men and women pray in separate rooms in the mosque. Women dress to cover their arms, legs, and hair. It's entirely possible that Muslims from the Gulf have spent almost none of their lives around the opposite sex apart from direct family members. Coming to the West is a shock!

This leads to a common misunderstanding. An American thinks they are trying to be friendly, while a Muslim international student thinks they are romantically interested. The differences in how men and women relate in Muslim versus Western cultures are significant enough that it is wisest to simply avoid them. Build friendships as men with men, and women with women, and be conscious of your comments and behavior with the opposite sex to avoid sending the wrong message.

The differences in how men and women relate in Muslim versus Western cultures are significant enough that it is wisest to simply avoid them. Build friendships as men with men, and women with women.

Some American Christians are troubled by women wearing hijabs (or more extensive coverings) or by perspectives on gender they perceive as repressive. Indeed, in some cultures these are signs of true oppression. But when is it right to speak up? As cultural outsiders our understanding of Muslim norms is very limited. Some women feel hijabs protect them from leering. And many Muslims have told me that with our lax morality and high divorce rates, the West—sadly, including Christians—hardly should be criticizing others. What you *can* do is focus on your own example. Speak and act in ways that honor the opposite gender. If they share them, listen empathetically to your friends' struggles. And share stories of how Jesus treated both women and men.

▶ CONCLUSION: WHEN A MUSLIM INTERNATIONAL STUDENT ARRIVES...

When Muslim international students arrive in their new country they are, like all travelers, a ball of contradictions.

Outwardly, they probably fit in with others on campus. Muslim youth are high technology users, every bit as addicted to their smartphones as Westerners. They are part of the emerging "global youth culture" whereby ubiquitous social media access spreads fashion and trends worldwide. So they may dress similarly, follow the same soccer teams (You follow soccer, right? If not, time to start!) and know the same musical artists you do. But internally they feel pushed and pulled in two directions.

The first is tradition. Ringing in their ears is advice from parents, uncles, and cousins about how to navigate their new surroundings well. Knowing the privilege it is to study in the West, they feel obligated to succeed at

school and eventually land a good job (here or in their own country). They want to bring honor to their family and community back home. They miss favorite foods, best friends, and even the smells and sounds of home. They have been warned about the corruption and immorality of the "Christian" West, and even about zealous Christians.

The second is freedom. They are excited about the new ideas and unparalleled consumer choice before them. It's been said, rather crudely, that when Muslim men from rigid Islamic countries arrive in the US to study there are two places they want to visit: a strip club and a church. These represent the opposite ends of the spectrum. Liberated from former rules, they can indulge in loose living like prodigals fresh from the father's home, or simply slack off in mosque attendance with fewer eyes watching. They can also ask questions about faith that were not permitted back home. In short they are looking for new experiences, new friends, and new ideas.

In 1948 an Egyptian named Sayyid Qutb came to the US as an international student, wondering if he would hold to Islam or embrace something new. While here he was shocked by immorality, materialism, and perceived shallowness, and returned to Egypt a vehement critic of the West and Christianity. Qutb's writing would inspire the founders of the Muslim Brotherhood, whose ideology influences radical Islam to the present day.

But what if while here Qutb had met believers who were culturally sensitive and whose lives reflected Jesus' goodness? How might history be different today if Qutb's time as an international student ended well?

This is the astonishing opportunity in connecting with international students: to meet those who will shape God's wide world for good or for harm. In the first portion of this handbook, we have looked to the example of Jesus our leader, surveyed key eras in Muslim-Christian history, and learned some of the layers of Muslim identity. With a deeper appreciation of our friends and greater wisdom for relating with them, we are now ready to get into the specifics of building gospel friendships with Muslims.

KEY POINTS

- The oneness of God, angels, holy books, prophets, judgment, and divine determinism are Islam's six core beliefs.
- The five pillars, or core practices, of Islam are the declaration of faith, prayer, giving alms, fasting, and pilgrimage.
- Sunni and Shi'a are the two main branches of Islam.
- Honor and shame, communal identity, and fear and power are parts of most Muslims' lives.
- Muslim men and women are accustomed to greater separation and more conservative roles than in the West.
- Muslim international students in the West often feel pulled in two directions: tradition and freedom.

ACTION STEP

Journal, comparing Muslim beliefs and cultural elements from this chapter, and your own background. Where might you have natural connections to Muslims? Where are you very different, and what do you need to be and do to adapt?

PRAYER

Heavenly Father, Praise you for your masterful creativity in making all the people of this world! Bless you for the diversity of cultures represented among Muslim peoples, and the biblical values like honor, family, and hospitality that they hold so dearly. I respect Muslims as people searching for you, though you are not far from any one of us (Acts 17:27), even as I pray that they will discover fullness of life and peace in Jesus Christ. Help me bring my own culture and background into relationships with Muslims, and give me a deeper understanding of their cultures and values, that I may represent you well in witness. In Jesus' name, Amen.

4 BUILDING GOSPEL FRIENDSHIPS

Hiba from the Gulf wanted to get her master's but needed to improve her English. She signed up for a language partner and was paired with Lydia, a Christian. The two spent hours together over coffee, shopping, walking, and talking about faith. Lydia answered Hiba's many questions with personal vulnerability and verses from the Bible. Eventually Hiba was accepted to a university across the country. Before she moved, she told Lydia, "You have loved me like family." Lydia replied, "The love I have comes from Jesus."

MEETING MUSLIMS

I'm sorry to say that even though there are many Muslims in my country, and I see them around my own neighborhood, I have never truly befriended one.

- A European international student in the US

"The first day you meet, you are friends. The next day you meet, you are brothers."

- Afghan proverb

If you are uncertain where to meet Muslim international students, take a Christian friend and walk around your campus, praying for God to guide you. Explore different departmental buildings and quads to see where people hang out. Men may be playing soccer, and women may frequent the closest coffee shop. Break the ice by being warm and inquisitive. Say *"Salaam alaykum,"* peace to you, the universal Muslim greeting. You may also try visiting an MSA meeting or international student club, provided they are open to guests. Most mosques and Islamic centers near campus are as well. Friday around noon is *jumma*, the central gathering time for Muslims.

Once, while visiting two Christian students on their campus, we came upon a large group of students milling around outside the TESOL (Teaching English to Speakers of Other Languages) building. As we walked through the crowd and heard many different languages, I asked one student what they were speaking. "Arabic," he responded and told me he and his friends were new students from Saudi Arabia. One of the Christians asked a question about their experience adapting to the school, and they immediately launched into conversation. Ten minutes later the break time had ended, but our new friends lingered with us. The group swapped numbers and made plans to get together soon. Seem too easy to be true? I have experienced it many times.

"Ten minutes later the break time had ended, but our new friends lingered with us."

If your campus group uses an info table, consider what may catch the eye of Muslims passing by. InterVarsity created "Love Your Muslim Neighbor" t-shirts at one particularly unwelcoming moment for Muslim internationals, and they became one of our best outreach tools! On one campus, Muslims snapped selfies with Christians wearing them. On another, the shirts sparked conversation at the nearby MSA (Muslim Student Association) table, and the two groups made plans to partner on a student event.

Practical acts of service, like making grocery runs with international students and helping them navigate the systems of US life, are deeply meaningful. One Christian said, "I helped a Lebanese student get eyeglasses one year, and her parents called from back home to thank me. Their response was overwhelming: the family bought me plane tickets to come visit them over the summer!"

أحبب جارك المسلم

LOVE YOUR MUSLIM NEIGHBOR

InterVarsity

"LOVE YOUR MUSLIM NEIGHBOR" OUTREACH

This interactive outreach station (which InterVarsity calls a Proxe) helps you welcome and get to know Muslim international students on campus and prompts you to share how Jesus responds to neighbors through the story of the Good Samaritan. Detailed instructions are online (tiny.cc/lymn-proxe). T-shirts with "Love Your Muslim Neighbor" in Arabic and English (tiny.cc/lymn) can be used with the Proxe or worn anytime: school, church, family gatherings...

You may not get an international plane ticket, but many Muslims who receive our hospitality are moved by experiencing Christian love that defies their expectations. This is a common thread of many students' testimonies. One brother testified that in a deeply painful chapter of life several years into his studies in the US, he realized that it was his Christian friends whom he could count on. This is when he realized he wanted to follow Jesus, too.

▶ HOSPITALITY AND VISITS

Visit your new friends' homes and welcome them into yours. In hospitality-oriented cultures, receiving guests is an almost sacred duty. There is an Arabic saying that "The guest is God's guest." Is this true of your culture as well? Consider this test: if you have learned a phrase like "After three days, fish and company stink" or expect guests to plan a time to visit in advance, you should get ready for change. In many Middle Eastern cultures visiting spontaneously indicates true friendship, since friends are always welcome. Reject a student who calls or shows up unexpectedly and you may signal that you are not interested in being friends. A classic international student complaint is that Americans require two weeks' notice to get together!

> During Ramadan, Victoria and her friends took a Libyan student some flowers and an umbrella late one rainy evening. She had been crying because she missed her mother yet was elated to see the guests. Victoria realized that she was on a video call with her mother right then! The mother thanked these visitors and said, "I didn't know there were Americans like this." And the student asked Victoria, "Are you really Christians, or are you angels?"

If you are invited into a Muslim friend's home, treasure the opportunity and leave several hours open. Bring a small gift like coffee or chocolate. You may have the chance to meet their roommates and expand your connections. If you are the host, provide food and drinks, and serve them to your friends.

Paying can be complicated. From a Muslim perspective, it is customary for locals to pay for the guest in coffee shops or restaurants the first time and most of the time. In our case, that means the American paying for the international student. But if you always pay it introduces imbalance to the relationship which may lead to your friend being shamed and withdrawing. Instead, alternate who pays, being sensitive to the cost involved. A simple cup of coffee or tea is all you need for a great conversation!

In Azerbaijan, I enjoyed an evening out with eight local guys. I wanted to show my appreciation, so I slipped away and paid the bill midway through the meal. I was unaware how significant the loss of face would be. When they found out at the end of dinner, I told them I was glad to pay, but they were so adamant I realized there would be a physical confrontation with the waiter if he did not return my money. I relented, my friends paid for me, and balance was restored to the universe.

CULTURAL DOS AND DON'TS OF INTERACTING WITH MUSLIMS

DOS	DON'TS
• Invite them into your home and practice warm hospitality.	• Don't eat pork or drink alcohol around them.
• Accept invitations to their homes, bring a gift, and remove your shoes upon entering.	• Don't shake hands with the opposite gender, unless they offer first.
• Pay for coffee/tea/meals (most of the time) if you are the inviter.	• Don't debate American foreign policy or Israel/ Palestine.
• Ask them about their home culture: food, family, traditions...	• Don't set firm time limits to your hangouts together.
• Stick with male-male and female-female interactions, especially in private.	• Don't eat in front of them without sharing.

▶ THE 5(+1) PILLARS OF GOSPEL FRIENDSHIPS

How can we grow our ordinary friendships into *spiritual* friendships and help our friends learn about Jesus? Picture a fleet of ships, both large and small—sailboats, cruise ships, speedboats, and rowboats. They represent the incredible diversity of the Muslim world. By embracing the following five key practices (which spell SHIPS), plus one extra, you will build faith-filled relationships with the Muslims in your life.

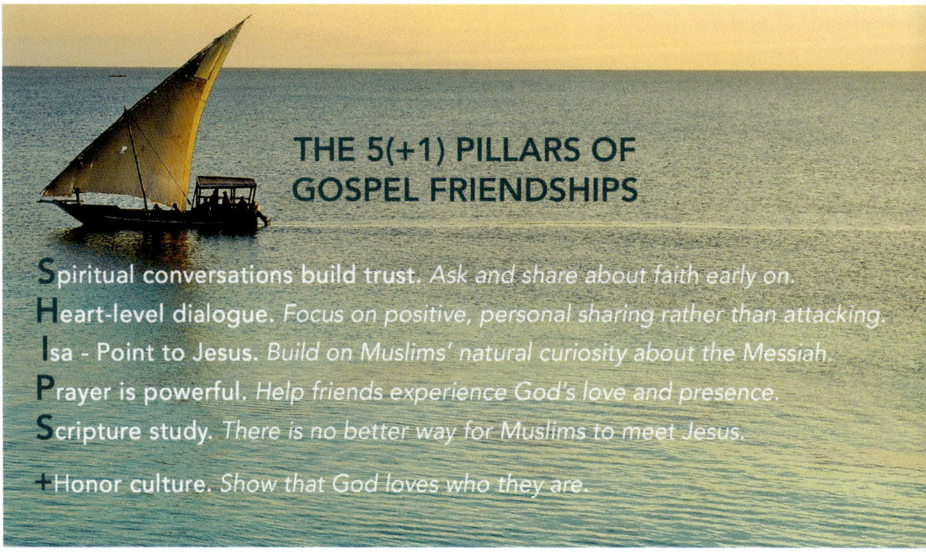

SPIRITUAL CONVERSATIONS BUILD TRUST.

> *These commandments that I give you today are to be on your hearts. … Talk about them when you sit at home and when you walk along the road, when you lie down and when you get up. Tie them as symbols on your hands and bind them on your foreheads.*
>
> *Deuteronomy 6:6-8*

"Since coming to America I have noticed that so many people are godless, atheists," Samira said. "Then I met you. I am so glad that you are a genuine believer like me!"

One Muslim student remarked to his American friend, "It's been six months since we've known each other, and only now you tell me about your belief in God? Is he not very important to you?"

Here in the West, bringing up God in conversations too early can turn people off, so many say to be patient and build trust first. If waiting to talk about faith irks you, ministry among Muslims is a breath of fresh air. That is because having spiritual conversations with Muslims *builds trust.*

Deuteronomy 6:4-9 is the Shema, Israel's statement of allegiance to Yahweh. The Lord commands his people to display their faith everywhere, so everyone around them knows about it. The Shema lifestyle is an invitation to make clear that we love and follow God by testifying often, in small and large ways.

Your faith is the center of your identity (hopefully!), and with Muslims, you are invited to be yourself. If another Christian asks "How's life?" you mention ways you are seeing—or seeking—God's guidance. As fellow people of faith, Muslims are accustomed to talking about God—remember how often your friend says "*inshallah*"? So we can be this open with them, too.

Your faith is the center of your identity, and with Muslims, you are invited to be yourself.

Be intentional to find or make opportunities. When someone asks what you did today, mention your devotional time in the Bible and prayer. Or lead with it, offering "I read something really insightful this morning..." When asked, "How are you?" answer, "I'm thanking God for this beautiful day!" Or if you are having an awful day, say, "This day has been terrible, but I am choosing to trust God because he has never failed me."

Like attracts like, so identifying yourself as a spiritual person draws Muslims who are also genuinely seeking God, as with Samira above. In this way, the Shema lifestyle is a great way to find other people who want to have spiritual conversations. Show that you are a safe person with whom to discuss matters of the heart, and your friends will come to you to talk. Show that you experience God's goodness, peace and power daily, and your friends will want to be around you to experience it, too.

Living this way does not mean that we become hokey super-spiritual stereotypes. I once knew a pastor who always answered, "How are you?" with an emphatic "Fabulous!" (Really? Every day?) Faith is displayed both through expressing gratitude for God's gifts and in *how* we lament struggles. With practice, you can be yourself and insert—or rather, not edit out—spiritual perspectives in just about every conversation.

HEART-LEVEL DIALOGUE

In my first year connecting with Muslims, I had a lot of one-time coffees. A new friend and I would meet in a coffee shop to get to know each other, and inevitably the conversation would move to spiritual topics. I loved debating theological points between our faiths. I thought my questions and arguments, delivered with a smile, would sow seeds of doubt and open them to new ideas. And perhaps at times they did! But then they ghosted me and did not return my calls and texts. One-time coffees.

A quick YouTube search confirms that plenty of Muslims and Christians believe attacking the other religion is the way to win people over. This is head-level dialogue. "Don't you realize the Trinity is illogical?" "Do you know the truth about Muhammad's lifestyle?" These often lead to arguments, and so can kill budding friendships. I am dismayed at the number of Christian trainings that teach complex apologetics to audiences new to ministry among Muslims. It is like putting the keys to a Tesla in the hands of a new driver: the risk of costly damage is too high.[52]

Here is a general rule: how deep you can delve into tense topics corresponds to how much trust you have built. Long-time friendship? You can probably talk about anything. Someone you met just this month? If the conversation gets tense, they will likely dig their heels in and fight back... or simply disappear. Without the relational security of a deep friendship very few people will listen to a critique of their religion. Fewer still will actually reflect on it. Within InterVarsity, our experience is that most Jesus-followers from Muslim backgrounds describe a process where their heart was warmed by the love and wisdom of Christ so that they wanted more and more of him. As this increased, their objections faded, to be dealt with later with the Spirit's help.

Early on in your relationships, aim for heart-level rather than head-level dialogue. Ask "What does being Muslim mean to you?" and "What do you experience when you pray?" Then share from your own heart. The Peace Feast is a flexible, scalable event that helps Muslims and Christians share food and heart-level dialogue about life and faith. Across the US and internationally, Peace Feasts are helping grow gospel friendships. Learn more in appendix B and plan one on your campus.

PEACE FEAST "HEART-LEVEL DIALOGUE" QUESTIONS (SEE APPENDIX B)

1. Share your name, major, background, and something you love about your culture/country.
2. Tell about a person who has played an important role in your faith journey. How did they influence you?
3. Tell about one of the faith practices that you enjoy (prayer, fasting, study, worship, community…).
4. What do you experience when you participate?
5. What is one of your favorite stories from your holy book, and why?
6. What is the central message or main goal of your faith, and how is it relevant to students on our campus?
7. What is it like being a Muslim/Christian in the United States right now? What's something about your faith that is often misrepresented by the media, and you would like us to understand?
8. Are you interested in learning about other religious traditions? If so, what aspects interest you and why?

ISA - POINT TO JESUS.

> While visiting a new town, a colleague and I stopped by the local mosque. It was deserted, save for an Iraqi man who greeted us at the door. After pleasantries he burst out with "Do you know what's wrong with Christianity?" GK Chesterton's words came to mind, "Sir, I am,"[53] but I listened and he said that Jesus never intended for the church to worship him. My mind began preparing a response to set his history straight, but then I thought, "I've just met this man and will probably never see him again. How productive will it be to spar with him?" Instead I asked, "Can I tell you a story Jesus told?" His face lit up. "Certainly!" I recited the parable of the Good Samaritan and said that we want to follow Jesus' example by being good neighbors to Muslims in his community.

Cross-cultural communication is a two-way street, shaped not only by the words spoken but how they are understood by the listener. If I say "Nazi," "hipster," or "cat meme," very specific images and associations come to your mind immediately. As we saw in chapters 2 and 3, the word "Christianity" has a cluster of negative connotations for Muslims: imperialism, polytheism, immoral, anti-family, Western/white religion. Students often tell me, "Our conversations got to the point of 'Islam teaches...' and 'Christianity teaches...' but then things kind of stalled out." No surprise there. Frame the conversation as my religion against yours and both sides make their points, disagree, and walk away.

While "Christian" is a minefield, Jesus is not. Muslims already love and respect **Isa al Masih**, *Jesus the Messiah.*

But while the word "Christian" is a minefield, Jesus is not. Muslims already love and respect *Isa al Masih*, Jesus the Messiah. In the Qur'an, Isa is called the word of God, the Messiah, and a sign and spirit from God. He is born of a virgin, is sinless, heals the sick, raises the dead, is alive in heaven, knows the judgment day, and commands our obedience. Amazing! Yet despite this high praise the Qur'an contains very little of Jesus' actual words and teachings, so Muslims are often curious to hear more.

> *I want my Muslim friend to walk with Jesus on the hills of Judea, sit with him by the Sea of Galilee, listen to him teach, watch him do miracles, hear him pray, talk with him, see him crucified and*

> *watch him come to the upper room alive on Resurrection Sunday. I want my Muslim friend to experience Jesus first. ... Biblical Christianity is not a dogma to be learned. It is first of all a personal relationship with Jesus.*[54]
>
> *- Sobhi Malek*

Telling stories of Jesus' words and deeds is one of the most valuable practices in friendships with Muslims. Ask, "Can I tell you something Jesus said/did?" and very few Muslims will respond, "No." This is a good way to detour around a controversial topic raised at an inopportune time, like with the man at the mosque. See the special section, Jesus in Everyday Conversations, to learn a simple way to connect Jesus to the topics you and your friends are already discussing.

Choosing the right Jesus stories can help your friend move toward Him. Early on, show your friend that Jesus' wisdom is accessible and relevant to our lives. Everyone can relate to worry in Matthew 6, and the invitation to seek first the kingdom of God challenges us all to consider our priorities. As your friend grows more familiar with Jesus' words, challenging words need to be heard like Jesus' statement "I am the way and the truth and the life. No one comes to the Father except through me" (John 14:6).

"But what if a story I tell falls flat?" Of course our friends will not respond eagerly every time. This is a risk we should be happy to take. I would rather be known as the guy who's always telling Jesus stories than to remain silent and miss chances to share good news.

JESUS IN EVERYDAY CONVERSATIONS
LEARNING TO HAVE SPONTANEOUS BIBLE STUDIES

1. **THINK OF SOME OF THE TOPICS THAT COME UP** almost any time you are with Muslim friends, or that students anywhere are concerned with. Examples: worry, career and success, love and relationships, politics, partying, sports.

2. **WHAT DOES JESUS HAVE TO SAY THAT RELATES TO THIS TOPIC?** If it's not immediately obvious, consider the underlying issue. Jesus didn't talk about dating, but the root issue may be a desire to be loved or wondering if we'll ever feel accepted. Examples:
   - *Worry*: Luke 12:22-34 "But seek his kingdom..."
   - *Career, success, professional sports*: Mark 8:36 "What good is it for someone to gain the whole world, yet forfeit their soul?"
   - *Loneliness, depression*: Matthew 11:28-30 "Come to me, all you who are weary...my burden is light."
   - *Facing our flaws*: Mark 2:17 "It is not the healthy who need a doctor, but the sick..."

3. **HOW HAS JESUS' TEACHING ON THIS TOPIC AFFECTED YOU?** What testimony can you give about how his wisdom has influenced your life and decisions?

4. **PRACTICE SHARING IT IN THIS THREE-PART STRUCTURE.**
   a. "Jesus said something interesting about that..."
   b. "Here's how it affects me..."
   c. "What do you think about that?"

Examples

Friend: "I'm really stressed out about these finals..."
You: "You know, Jesus said something interesting about that. He said God already knows our worries and wants to take care of us. Rather than be consumed by anxiety, we should prioritize God's kingdom first and then he will help other things find their place. That's challenging to me, but I am trying to live my life this way: I seek God and I ask him for help. [example] And as I place my spiritual life first, I really do find that the other pieces fit in their place. But what about you...what do you think about that?"

Friend: "The government/that politician is so wicked..."
You: "I get discouraged by corrupt systems too, like ____... But Jesus said something interesting about that which

challenges me. He said, 'Don't point out the speck of dust in someone else's eye while ignoring a board stuck in your own eye!' His point was that when we fixate on everyone else's issues, we often ignore our own. If I'm honest, the same things that bother me in those politicians—selfishness, greed, pride—are in me, too! [example] So I pray and ask God to work on my heart first, not just fix everyone else. What do you think about that?"

You just had a spontaneous Bible study! Depending on how the ensuing conversation goes, you can ask "Would you like to read more about Jesus in the *Injil* (Gospel)?"

5. **PREPARE SEVERAL OF THESE AND USE THEM OFTEN!** Doing your homework ahead of time helps you recognize opportunities (1 Peter 3:15) and share more naturally.

PRAYER IS POWERFUL

> Our small group's prayer time was about to begin when one member came in with her Muslim friend. "Amal has been having a hard time at home, and I said we would be happy to pray for her." We asked if we could lay hands on her and spent several minutes in fervent prayer that God would give peace to her family. When we finished Amal had tears in her eyes. "While you were praying, I could feel heat through your hands!" she said. "I experienced that once before when Christians prayed for me, and it is wonderful." My friend replied, "That's because when we pray in Jesus' name, God acts. You were feeling his love for you."

Across InterVarsity, Muslim international students are becoming curious about, growing closer to, and even coming to faith in Jesus through prayer. We don't just pray *for* Muslims; we pray *with* Muslims and the Spirit often shows up. Prayer is the primary way we can help our friends experience God's love and presence.

Prayer and the supernatural are significant to Muslims. Our friends are generally quite open to us praying for them. In two decades of ministry, no Muslim has ever declined my offer of prayer! Most believe that dreams and visions convey truth. According to one *hadith*, Muhammad promised visions after he was gone as a form of revelation.[55] Many cultures have elaborate books on dream interpretation.

Prayer is intimate and can help soften hearts. The act of praying for a person honors them and is a show of caring friendship. Honor/shame, hospitality-oriented cultures value both of these gestures. Often our spiritual conversations hit up against theological and cultural obstacles. But if a friend experiences the Spirit's presence through prayer, as did Amal, it can jumpstart a personal search for Jesus.

Considering these points, here are some ways to use prayer more.

Be courageous and lead with prayer when meeting people. Try prayer walking, asking God to lead you to Muslims. If your campus group has an info table out, offer prayer to passersby. Say, "We're praying for students' needs. Is there something we can pray for you about?" And when you visit a Muslim's home, ask, "May I offer a prayer of blessing for your family and this place?" You could speak it or bring the blessing in a gift, like an artfully calligraphed, framed verse. Consider a blessing of wisdom and guidance like Jeremiah 17:7-8 or even Jesus' words like Matthew 6:33-34.

We can respond to our friends' needs through prayer, as well. If someone mentions physical, emotional, or social needs, don't just listen. Respond right then! Pray to God, and close asking all things in Jesus' name. Like Amal, many experience God's power through physical contact. If you're of the same gender, put a hand on their shoulder or take their hands in yours. As Rawson said, even when there is no dramatic healing, Jesus' presence in prayer often moves people.[56]

If you have a sense that someone is under spiritual attack like demonism or curses, use the spiritual authority that is ours in Christ to pray against it.

THE POWER OF PRAYER

Janice listened to Alima tell of the terrifying nightmares and physical pain she'd been experiencing for the past two weeks. "That sounds like some kind of spiritual attack. When I pray in Jesus' name, God acts," Janice said. "May I pray for you?" Laying hands on her friend, she asked God to show Alima his love and protection. They didn't see each other for the next week, but when they did Alima tearfully exclaimed, "The nightmares stopped!" Janice celebrated, but also urged her friend to invite Jesus to make his home in her heart permanently.

Unless you have been trained in prayer ministry, you may want to ask an experienced friend for help with this.[57] And a power encounter should be coupled with an invitation to accept Jesus, because lasting protection comes only to those indwelt by the Holy Spirit (Matthew 8:16, John 14:12, Matthew 12:43-45).

Similarly, after a person comes to faith, their discipleship may be hindered by wounds and sinful past deeds. With a trusted Christian partner, take time to pray with the new believer through these issues, renouncing them and inviting Jesus to shine his light in every corner of their life.

Finally, recognize that you may experience spiritual attack. Sometimes after an intense conversation or spiritual encounter, I go home feeling inordinately discouraged, depressed, or just gross. Some call this "being slimed." Ask a trusted friend to pray for cleansing and protection for you. Pray words of scripture and listen to worship music to remind yourself of God's truth. When we're on the front lines the enemy aims his attacks at us, but He who is in us is greater (1 John 4:4).

SCRIPTURE STUDY

> A Franco-North African friend was Muslim on his father's side only and decided that he should become "more Muslim." He started reading the Qur'an, but quickly found that he wanted to know more about *Isa*, Jesus. He began reading the Gospels and was amazed at the detailed stories of Jesus' words and life found only in the Bible. Ultimately his Bible reading brought him to faith in Christ.

Studying Scripture with Muslims is the topic of the entire next chapter, so for now we will simply note its importance for gospel friendships. In InterVarsity, *every* outreach effort and conversation with Muslims is a step toward opening the Scriptures. There is no better way for an international student to meet Jesus than through the Bible, through which the Spirit speaks directly to our hearts. Why try to summarize and explain it by my own words when I can open *the* Word and invite my friend to see for themselves?

There is no better way for an international student to meet Jesus than through the Bible.

WHEN YOUR MUSLIM FRIEND HAS A DREAM...

Pastoring Supernatural Encounters with Jesus

Dreams and visions are significant to Muslims, and the Lord is using them to draw people to himself both on campus and around the world. Most Muslims are attuned to these kinds of supernatural experiences. Having a dream doesn't mean your friend is seeking... but it may mean God is seeking them. So how can we join what God's doing and guide Muslim friends closer to Jesus?

In general...

ASK ABOUT DREAMS WHEN GETTING TO KNOW MUSLIMS.

- *"Have you ever had a dream where you felt God was trying to send you a message?"*
- *"Have you ever had a dream of Jesus?"*

This is a good way to find people who are already opening up spiritually. Even if your friend has not had such a dream, the door's open to ask, *"Do you believe God uses dreams?"* Share about any of your own such experiences, if you have had any.

If your friend mentions a dream...

1. AFFIRM THEIR EXPERIENCE.

- *"Wow, that's tremendous! I believe God uses dreams to communicate truth."*
- *"I know of other people who have also had powerful dreams. God used them to bring amazing changes to their lives."*

Muslim international students have had dreams and visions of Jesus inviting them to find him during their time in the US, Jesus restoring brokenness, Jesus calming their fears, and Jesus calling them to follow him. Countless others around the world have similar experiences.

2. ASK ABOUT THE DREAM AND THEIR EXPERIENCE OF IT.

- *"What happened in your dream? Please tell me all about it! ... How did you feel when...?"*

3. INTERPRET.

- *"What do you think your dream means? What do you think God is trying to tell you?"*

Ask the Spirit to give you discernment about the meaning of their dream. With sensitivity to your friend and to the Spirit, this is a time to be bold!

- *"It seems clear that God wants you to learn new things about himself..."*
- *"I think God's trying to get your attention..."*

4. LOOK FOR SCRIPTURE CONNECTIONS.

Are there images or words of Jesus that correspond with the dream? Share them.

- *"I have studied the Injil (Gospel) deeply, and there is a connection to your experience..."*

Jesus bringing comfort - Matthew 11:28
Jesus in white - Mark 9:2-13
Doors or gates - Matthew 7:7-8, 13-14, John 10, Revelation 3:20
Houses, rooms, paths, Jesus preparing a place - John 14:1-7

5. OFFER PRACTICAL STEPS FORWARD.

- *"Would you like to ask Jesus to show you the way forward right now?"*
- *"Let's read the Gospel together and learn Jesus' message to us."*

This step could be listening prayer, reading the Bible together, or an invitation to put their trust in Jesus right then. Whatever it is, lay hands on them, bless the work God is doing, and invite him to continue revealing his will to them.

HONOR CULTURE

International student ministry can subconsciously package Jesus in an American box. Every international student is changed by their experience abroad, learning new cultural styles and norms. There is a struggle re-entering one's home country even in the best of cases. Try searching "reverse culture shock." But when American Christians minister to internationals in the same way they do to other Americans—and this is precisely what comes naturally—we export cultural add-ons and teach students not to be Indonesian, Iranian, or Indian for Christ as God intends, but to be American. This produces disciples who see their background not as part of God's story, but as something to be rejected for the "better" ways of the West. Sounds a lot like colonialism.

The Jerusalem council of Acts 15 decreed that Gentiles do not need to adopt Jewish culture in order to follow Jesus. Lamin Sanneh, Gambian missiologist and believer from a Muslim background, described a pattern of cultural diversity since the dawn of Christianity. In contrast to Islam, which privileges Arabic as the divine language, the New Testament was written in the widely used Greek rather than the Aramaic that Jesus spoke. From Hebrew culture to Hellenistic culture, on to European, African, Asian, and Latin American cultures, each of which brought their own flavor to Christianity, *translation is God's way* of spreading his message.[58]

> *No culture is so advanced and so superior that it can claim exclusive access or advantage to the truth of God, and none so marginal and remote that it can be excluded. All have merit, none is indispensable.*[59]
>
> *- Lamin Sanneh*

It is impossible to share a culture-less gospel with our Muslim friends. But from the moment we meet them, we can celebrate our friends' cultures and by doing so show that the God we worship loves who they are. Ask questions about their country's history and present and listen with a desire to learn. Ask what they value and miss from back home. Try new foods. Listen to their music. Attend cultural events with them. Each of these small actions add up to honor our friends and help prepare for them to develop culturally appropriate faith, a topic to which we will return in chapter 7.

And please, do not whitewash the history and present of the USA. International students are sharp enough to appreciate the good while also facing the truth of our country's racism and oppression. I once attended an international student event where these very topics came up. "That sounds like my country, too," was a repeated comment, and it opened the door to talk about the pervasiveness of sin across all cultures.

BUILDING GOSPEL FRIENDSHIPS WITH MUSLIM WOMEN (WRITTEN BY A FEMALE TEAMMATE)

Meeting Muslim women is a joy! When I met Zehra, I was immediately struck by her beauty, peacefulness, and very stylish clothing. Her English was limited, but we found our way through conversation, usually laughing at ourselves and asking her children to interpret.

Zehra was a generous host. Once she invited my family over to her apartment and I was amazed to see that she had cooked six different Turkish dishes for us to enjoy!

As trust grew, our conversations went deeper. I had been praying for opportunities to share faith when Zehra surprised me by suddenly asking, "What is paradise?" Silently praising God, I was able to share with her the Christian viewpoint of what happens after death for those who believe in Jesus as Lord.

Of course, not all Muslim women are just like Zehra. But most have similarities. All of the Muslim women I have known are incredibly hospitable, very proud of their culture and beliefs, and love to spend lots of time together. Friendships have the potential to last a lifetime. When we have the chance to look deeply, we will see that many women are carrying heavy fears and questions about where to find hope and healing.

Appearance is very important to Muslim women. Headscarves, clothing, even perfumes and make-up are carefully chosen. Instead of making assumptions about what this means, gently ask questions. Remember that your own modesty will be appreciated and can be a factor your Muslim friend uses to determine if she will introduce you to her husband, male relatives, or friends.

KEY POINTS

- Meet Muslims by being creative, warm, and flexible. Serving internationals practically can open doors.
- Practice generous hospitality and be a good guest, as these are important in Muslim cultures.
- Use the acronym "SHIPS+" to remember key principles for gospel friendships:
    - **S**piritual conversations build trust.
    - **H**eart-level dialogue.
    - **I**sa - Point to Jesus.
    - **P**rayer is powerful.
    - **S**cripture study.
    - +Honor culture.

ACTION STEP

Make a plan for how you can make a Muslim friend or broaden and deepen your current relationships, and act on it this week. Bring your faith into those relationships as a natural part of sharing who you are, offering Jesus stories and prayer.

PRAYER

Dear Lord, In your divine wisdom you have brought Muslim international students here from every corner of the world. Thank you for the privilege of befriending them! Prepare the people you will introduce me to, for you go before me. Speak to them in dreams and through prayer, and open their hearts, for you are the God who seeks us. Help me serve and be hospitable, for you are a welcoming God. Give me courage to share how you bring hope and peace into my life, for you are worth sharing. And deepen my own prayer life, that I may know you more deeply, depend on you more fully, and minister in the Spirit's power. In the name of the Father, the Son, and the Holy Spirit, Amen.

5 READING SCRIPTURE

There seems to me to have been twice as much done in some ages in defending the Bible as in expounding it, but if the whole of our strength shall henceforth go to the exposition and spreading of it, we may leave it pretty much to defend itself. ... Pardon me if I offer a quiet suggestion. Open the door and let the lion out; he will take care of himself.

- Charles Spurgeon

As he waited on the lawn outside the campus center, Jerome prayed. Mostly to calm his own nerves. Over the past two days since they discussed it at the Peace Feast, he'd spent a lot of time wondering what it would be like reading the Bible with Ishaq. The two had become friends playing pickup soccer, which led to video games, which led to late night conversations and drinking tiny cups of really strong tea—yet another new experience for Jerome, and still not as good as coffee. At the Peace Feast the two realized how many prophets are common to Islam and Christianity. Ishaq was intrigued by the longer narrative accounts of their lives in the Bible, and Jerome suggested they read some together. Fifteen minutes after Jerome sat down on the lawn, Ishaq arrived with his friend Farzad.

The discussion that day alternated between meandering and focused and was...really fun! Jerome was surprised at the similarities in the story of Joseph (or Yusuf, as Ishaq said) as told in the Bible and the Qur'an. At one point, Farzad seemed to be fishing for a debate, but Ishaq calmed his friend down and they returned to the passage at hand. Later Jerome caught sight of him flipping pages and reading ahead. And Jerome was glad for the lively conversation that the group dynamic brought. Most of all, it was powerful looking at biblical wisdom together and making connections to life today. Jerome knew this was the main event, and he looked forward to the next time.

There is no better place for Muslims to get to know Jesus than in the pages of Scripture. It is there that they meet Jesus in his refreshing approachability and compassion, razor sharp insight into human nature, unparalleled miracles, sacrifice on the cross and victorious resurrection. What we struggle to do with our own words, the Bible does for itself. Reading Scripture with Muslims is the main event. As the Spurgeon quote above says, let the lion out and it can take care of itself!

In this chapter we will share best practices for inviting Muslim friends to read Scripture together, and tips for good discussions. We will also unpack some of the differences in how Muslims and Christians approach our holy books.

▶ HOW TO INVITE

> *He taught them many things by parables, and in his teaching said: "Listen! A farmer went out to sow his seed. As he was scattering the seed..."*
>
> *Mark 4:2-4.*

> As I walked up the hill to the student dorm, my phone buzzed. "Ahmed says he can't make it to our Bible study," my friend said. "Oh no!" I said, dismayed. "I guess I'll just go home, then." My friend interrupted, "Actually, can you come anyway? I kind of invited a couple other Muslims I know who were nearby, and they want to read together. They just called their friends, and there are about seven people here now."

The worst mistake we make around reading Scripture with Muslims is to wait. We assume they will not be interested, or we imagine the invitation as a terrifying moment. For a variety of reasons our friends may *already* be curious about the Bible.

In the previous chapters we noted that the Qur'an identifies much of the Bible as holy revelation by God, credits Jesus with miracles beyond anything Muhammad performed, and commands believers to obey him (Q 3:49-50). Yet the Qur'an includes very little of Jesus' actual teachings and words, so many Muslims are curious to learn more. Even those who are suspicious about the integrity of the Bible are often willing to look for themselves.

A simple principle for inviting Muslims to read Scripture with you is this: Ask early, ask often, and let the Word do the work. We have zero desire to trick or manipulate our friends into belief in Jesus. Rather, like the apostle Paul, we set "forth the truth plainly" (2 Corinthians 4:2) to allow them to meet the real Christ and decide for themselves how to respond.

Not everyone you ask will say "yes," and not all who begin will continue, and that is ok. Fruitful Christians ministering among Muslims have *many* one-time Scripture discussions, a handful that last several meetings, and precious few that go the distance. Jesus' parable of the seeds in Mark 4 describes three out of four that do not last. But the one that does multiplies spectacularly. There is a colossal difference between the sower who scatters many seeds that never take root, and the one who never scatters at all. May we be generous, wide sowers and trust the Lord to bring his harvest.

…ng are four ways to invite Muslims to read Scripture with you. As you read them, ask yourself:

Which of these am I most comfortable with? If that were the only approach I used, how might it limit me?

1. INVITE FOLLOWING A JESUS STORY

"There are a lot of other interesting stories from Jesus' life. Would you like to read some of them together?"

As you live a "Shema lifestyle" (chapter 4), you will have opportunities to tell stories from Jesus' life and teachings relevant to everyday conversations. If you and your friend have an interesting, even brief, conversation, follow up right then with an invitation to keep reading. In fact, when you tell a Jesus story pull out your phone's Bible app and invite your friend to see the text for themselves.

2. INVITE A BRAND-NEW FRIEND

"I've heard that many international students would like to read the Bible but have never had the chance. I have one, and we're here now. Would you like to read it together?"

Consider asking a friend right at the beginning of your relationship, or even when you first meet them. While this approach may seem abrupt, it is possible to be both direct and sensitive. Muslims have been this direct inviting me to read the Qur'an, and I felt not offended, but valued.

3. INVITE AN OLD FRIEND

"You know my faith in Jesus is precious to me. I care about you, so I want to share what's precious to me with you..."

If you wait too long it can become more awkward to bring up faith, so we recommend doing so early. But it is possible to open new topics. Based on

MATTHEW 6:
A SPONTANEOUS BIBLE STUDY FOR ANYTIME, ANYWHERE

One passage that every Christian should be ready to share is Matthew 6:25-34. We live in an anxious age. Exams, relationships, health, injustice, political and economic instability, and more. Jesus' words about worry offer both comfort and challenge. So next time it comes up in a conversation, say "Can I share one of my favorite things Jesus said about that?" Then open the text and dig in!

the trust and care you have together, invite your friendship to a still-deeper level. This truly is what it means to know someone: to share in the things that we treasure most closely. You want the same from your Muslim friend, right?

4. INVITE FROM THE QUR'AN

"I've read that the Qur'an says believers should be familiar with all the holy books. Do you read the Tawrat, Zabur, and Injil?"

You can invite a friend based on the Qur'an's own invitation: "Believers, believe in Allah, his messenger, the book he revealed to his messenger, and the book he revealed beforehand. Whoever disbelieves in Allah, his angels, his books, his messengers, and the last day has gone far astray. (Q 4:136). See "Should I read the Qur'an?" below for more.

TIPS FOR INVITING WELL

Most Muslim cultures do spontaneity well. So, if God provides a moment of curiosity, seize it! If they agree to read the Scriptures with you, suggest beginning right then or tomorrow. If you are too rigid with your schedule ("I can meet Tuesdays at 1 pm") you might find that your friend is never available at your pre-planned time. I know a believer from a Muslim background who has marathon all-night reading sessions with his seeking friends.

Many people are hesitant to commit up front to meeting multiple times. But you do not have to say, "Can we meet for the next six months?" If you sense your friend is unsure, simply invite them to read once. When that finishes, suggest meeting again. Then repeat. The Bible is captivating, and one good story feeds interest in another.

Any time you invite someone, add, "Is there another friend you can invite to join us?" The Greek term *oikos* describes one's household, which in our case could be their family or trusted friends. Groups have livelier conversation, and as we discussed in chapter 3, communal cultures make decisions communally. If the *oikos* ultimately comes to trust Jesus together they will find identity, security, and accountability as a body. This is happening in ministry to other religious groups around the world. But let *them* indicate who they would like to invite, rather than you guessing and bringing together people who may not trust each other and if so will not open up.

Any time you invite someone, add, "Is there another friend you can invite to join us?"

You want to help your friend be at ease and able to engage fully. Ask where they would be comfortable meeting: in a home, coffee shop, on campus, or elsewhere. The New International Reader's Version (NIRV) is an excellent English translation for non-native speakers due to its clear style and simple vocabulary. Try to have both the English and their language (bible.com/languages)[60] on hand. As your reading progresses and they become more curious, gift them a Bible of their own.

BUT WHY NOT JUST INVITE THEM TO MY SMALL GROUP BIBLE STUDY?

If a Muslim friend is already attending your small group Bible study, go with it! Experiencing Spirit-filled community can be a powerful part of our witness. It is good for Muslims to see how Christians discuss and apply God's Word together. Talk with other Christians in your group, sharing tips from this handbook, to help them welcome and relate well to your friend. But if you have not yet begun, you should know that majority-Christian groups are not always the ideal place for a Muslim to read the Bible, for a number of reasons.

First, most small groups are full of "stuff American Christians do." These are not all bad, but we want to limit the cultural baggage that accompanies our gospel witness, to allow our friends to meet Jesus through their own cultural lenses.

Second, many Muslims are understandably cautious about reading the Bible. A small group that snaps selfies and posts everything online could threaten your friend's privacy. Even Muslims who are not concerned about this at the beginning may become concerned later on. We need to be cautious on our friends' behalf.

Third, a small group may not be studying the parts of the Bible most helpful for a seeker to begin with. Sometimes our friends are only open for a brief moment. We want them to see the big story, centered on Jesus. And they will bring a wide variety of questions, on and off topic, which we should be ready to accommodate.

For these reasons, it is usually best to explore faith in a separate Bible study. But if they are already in your existing small group, meet with them at other times to check in, debrief the experience, and engage their questions. You may even start a personal study on the side. Sure, this means more time and effort. Your friend is worth it!

MUSLIMS AND THE BIBLE

"What is one of your favorite stories from your holy book, and why?" was the question before my Peace Feast table group. "I enjoy the story of Ayub," a student from the Gulf said. He shared the brief Qur'anic account. I mentioned that this story (Job) occupies forty-two chapters of the Bible, and shared details about Job's interactions with his unhelpful friends. My new friends were riveted. "Do you know about Nuh (Noah), too?" Our conversation spun off into a delightful fifteen-minute tangent as we discussed him and other characters.

-CRIPTURE

at holy books with great reverence. Many evangelicals could ... some tips! A Qur'an is normally kept on the highest shelf and often wrapped in cloth. Some will not touch it or the Bible without washing their hands first, but you can use smartphones or printed handouts. Never place your Bible on the ground. You might want to use one without any underlining and notes written in it, though you can also explain that for many Christians, taking notes as we study the text is precisely how we revere God's Word.

Most Muslims do not read the Qur'an in the same ways Christians read the Bible. They usually listen to the Qur'an being recited and are not familiar with inductive study. Do not be discouraged if your friend is hesitant to ask questions at first. Over time as they realize this is a safe space to do so, they will ask many.

Muslims usually enjoy the biblical text. Through Islamic history much has been made of the supposed "miracle of the Qur'an" whereby no other book can match the beauty and style of the Arabic text (cf. Q 11:13-14). Of course, this claim cannot be objectively proven. But personal experience testifies that when Muslims dip into the rich narrative and relatable detail in the Bible, they are captivated.

The Qur'an is written in poetic style somewhat akin to the book of Proverbs, with sparse details and no context (later Islamic commentators supplied their own). The Bible sets historical context ("In the year King Uzziah died, I saw the Lord" in Isaiah 6), provides extra detail about characters beloved in Islam (as I relayed to my Peace Feast group about Job), and does not shy away from sin and brokenness (David's adultery, murder and then prayer of repentance in 2 Samuel 11-12 and Psalm 51). All of this makes for good reading!

Additionally, Muslim international students often relate to the Bible's Semitic cultures in ways Westerners do not. Be sure to welcome their input and questions, and you may learn something new.

▶ HOW TO READ TOGETHER

DISCOVERY BIBLE STUDY

There are far more right ways than wrong ways to read Scripture with Muslims. But one study method, Discovery Bible Study (DBS), was designed for cross-cultural witness and is central in numerous movements to Christ happening around the world today.

The DBS format is simple, which helps non-native English speakers follow along and share the story with others. Each discussion ends with the challenge to respond actively to the passage (John 13:17), wherever participants are in their journey. Sadly, response is often the part we Christians leave out when we read the Word!

Part of the DBS response is to tell the story to someone else in their life. Now, before coming to faith in Jesus, is actually the *best* time for a Muslim to begin sharing with others. By retelling small stories and bits of truth they are enjoying, they learn witness as a normal part of engaging with Scripture. And at this stage they engage other Muslims as fellow learners and part of the same community. Sometimes new DBS groups begin this way!

KEY PRINCIPLES OF DISCOVERY BIBLE STUDY

- Group studies in natural communities, where people are already connected as friends or family (non-Christians should be the majority whenever possible).
- Discovery, not teaching; facilitators, not "leaders." Let the Scripture lead the discussion and join in, rather than providing answers.
- Discipleship to conversion: Jesus brought the disciples into mission before they fully understood him, and DBS follows the same practice of helping people obey Jesus from the very beginning.

DBS STEPS

A. What are you thankful for right now? What are you stressed or worried about?
B. How did you do with the response last time? Who did you share the story with?
C. Read the passage out loud at least twice. Each person should then try to retell the passage without looking (others can help). Don't skip this part!
D. Discussion Questions:
   1. What's interesting, challenging, or confusing about this text?
   2. What does this story teach us about God? About people?
   3. What does this story teach us to do or obey? How will you respond?
   4. Who do you know who should hear this story this week?

STAYING ON TRACK

> It was my second time meeting with Farzad to read together, and we were about to finish the story of Noah and the flood. Out of nowhere he asked, "You Christians believe Jesus is God, right?" My mind raced to decide how to reply. "That, my friend, is a great question about an incredibly important point," I said. "But I've found it hard to explain Jesus' full identity with my words alone. Can we stay in this passage right now discussing Noah, and then when we get to Jesus you can see for yourself and decide who he is? We're going to get to the ***Injil*** soon, and when we do I promise not to hold back."

You may think my answer to Farzad was a missed opportunity. But many other times when I followed my friends' ping-ponging questions, we lost track of the current text, and the constructive conversation morphed into a debate neither they nor I were ready for.

Discovery takes time and walking alongside our friends requires many judgment calls. With prayerful discernment, you may sense whether your friend is asking a question out of genuine openness, or to bait you and sidetrack the conversation.

If I thought Farzad was genuinely open at that moment, we could have shifted and read a passage like John 14 right then. In that way he would still be discovering Jesus for himself, in the text. Muslims at the trust and curiosity threshold often—though not always—ask questions to test you, while those at the open and seeking thresholds ask to truly learn..

Muslims at the trust and curiosity threshold often ask questions to test you, while those at the open and seeking thresholds ask to truly learn.

DRAWING OUT GOSPEL THREADS

Choosing discovery over telling at early thresholds does not mean that you must sit silent until the text explicitly states an important point. The Bible is one unified story of God's redemption plan, and there are "gospel threads" woven throughout. As you and your friends read together, draw out these threads to help build the case for the gospel.

Two themes Muslims need to grasp are that sin is a greater problem than we think, and that salvation comes not by our own power but God's intervention.

The Islamic view of sin is milder than the Christian view. Islam does not teach original sin, but rather that humans are inherently weak and make poor choices. Even the term sin is unfamiliar to many Muslims, who refer more to bad deeds. Because the problem is not as serious, Muslims do not recognize the need for a savior.

Yet in practice, many Muslims feel deep shame and inadequacy before God. As you study Scripture, draw out how sin goes beyond deeds to the deep attitudes of the heart, creates a chasm between us and God, and ultimately can only be resolved by Him. David committed adultery and murder, and Psalm 51 contains one of the most poignant confessions of sin anywhere—and from a great prophet no less. "Against you, and you only have I sinned... Create in me a pure heart," he says to God.[61]

Images of how sin covers us with shame before others and God may be helpful (Isaiah 59:2, Ezra 9:6). Muslims also value cleanliness before God, so sin as defilement is also an appropriate image (Isaiah 64:6, Mark 7:15). You could illustrate how sin stains our character like a shirt with just a bit of blood on it, or tea with just a drop of spit in it!

Soon after the last conversation, Farzad and I studied Abraham and his son, in Genesis 22:1-14 and Qur'an 37:99-107. I asked how he wanted to apply this story, and Farzad said he wanted to obey God like Abraham. I affirmed this but pointed out that Abraham's obedience, by itself, was not enough to save him. The Qur'anic account says God "ransomed him with a great sacrifice," and in the Bible Abraham calls the place "The Lord will provide." We discussed what it means that our sin is too great a problem for us to fix by ourselves, and we need God's help, and I shared how this passage foreshadows Jesus ransoming us.[62]

▶ READING SCRIPTURE WITH MUSLIM WOMEN (WRITTEN BY A FEMALE TEAMMATE)

Once, I invited my friend Shirin to come to my house to read the Bible together. Shirin had grown up in a Muslim home but didn't know what to believe anymore. I shared one of my favorite scriptures with her: the story of Jesus on an important trip pausing to heal a bleeding woman in Mark 5. We read the story together and discussed her many questions. Near the end of our study time, I asked her, "Do you know anyone that needs healing?" With tearful eyes Shirin immediately answered, "Yes. Me!" She shared with me some of the deep emotional pain she was experiencing, and we prayed together on the spot.

When we give Muslim women opportunities to see the truth and beauty of Jesus for themselves, they have the opportunity to directly respond to and receive from him. How much better this is for them than to simply hear how Jesus impacted someone else! In a ministry where we hope to pass on tools that can be utilized when internationals return home, reading and responding to the Bible tops the list!

Jesus' interactions with women in the Bible highlight many wonderful truths, such as the way he elevates them in society, values their healing, draws them to himself, accepts them as followers and supporters, and

SHOULD I READ THE QUR'AN?

Some Muslims are open to reading with you, but hesitant to jump straight into the Bible. They would prefer that we read the Qur'an and the Bible side by side. This may be because of concerns about the Bible's integrity (see appendix C) or out of desire to teach us their book.

Meanwhile some Christians are hesitant to open the Qur'an, possibly because of negative messages they have heard about Islam. If a Muslim friend is willing to go straight into the Bible, we gladly go straight to the Bible. But if not, Christians should not hesitate to say yes to a Qur'an-and-Bible reading group. By doing so we extend our friends the same trust and vulnerability that we ask of them in opening our holy book. Reading the Qur'an does not mean you agree with everything written in it. Rather, you're following Paul's example in Athens by starting from what your audience already values and bridging to the full truth (Acts 17).

even cares for his own mother. Find these scriptures in appendix D and more on friendships with Muslim women in appendix E.

WHAT TO READ TOGETHER

InterVarsity has produced three Scripture series, plus a number of topical guides, to help you and your Muslim friends. Each of these can be found in appendix D.

WHO IS JESUS THE MESSIAH?

Each passage in this Bible study series from the book of Luke draws out a different aspect of Jesus' message, from its very beginning to the cross and resurrection. Gradually, they reveal the fullness of his identity.

JESUS' INTERACTIONS WITH WOMEN

Our Savior showed compassion to women and empowered them to follow

Two guidelines can help sensitive Christians engage with the Qur'an well:

Treat the Qur'an with respect. While no Muslim should expect a non-Muslim to venerate the Qur'an, you can speak kindly and avoid disparaging it. Most Muslims do not carry their holy book around, but if you handle one, do so carefully.

Resist the temptation to interpret the Qur'an for Muslims. Rather than offer your interpretation of what you think the Qur'an is trying to say, ask questions about how your friends understand and live out the text. Point out parallels to biblical passages, or areas of difference. It is certainly fine to disagree but do so from a position of humility.

Once, a frustrated Christian invited me to join him and four Muslim friends one evening. Their frequent spiritual conversations got hung up on a mutual distrust of the other's holy book. When we met, inevitably, faith came up. I had been reading the Qur'an, and knowing their hesitation to discuss the Bible, decided to go with it. "Guys, I have been reading Sura Al Imran (3). I am amazed at what it says about Isa! Healing the sick, raising the dead, and even creating life. This is far beyond any other prophet's miracles, right? I have to wonder: have you given enough consideration to who this Isa really is?" When I got home, I followed up with each of them individually, and one replied that he had been reflecting on our conversation and wanted to read the *Injil*.

him, a moving invitation to Muslim women. This series has fifteen stories of Jesus interacting with women in the Gospels.

SHARED PROPHETS: A QUR'AN/BIBLE DISCUSSION GUIDE

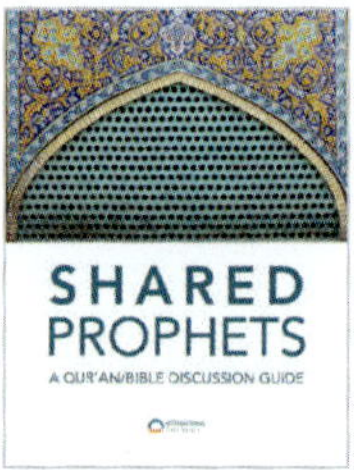

If you and your friends are planning to read the Qur'an and the Bible together, use "Shared Prophets: A Qur'an/Bible Discussion Guide." This series examines seven common prophets, from Adam to Jesus, showing that sacrifice is central to God's redemption plan.

PEACE FEASTS

In chapter 4 we introduced the Peace Feast, an event focused on sharing food and heart-level dialogue. InterVarsity's topical Peace Feast guides incorporate qur'anic and biblical passages relating to justice, friendship, prayer, suffering, fasting, love, thankfulness, and other topics. The Muslim perspectives and Qur'an passages included were either written or vetted by a number of Muslims so you can be confident they are used in good faith. These guides are a fantastic way to break into reading and discussing Scripture together on a level playing field for both groups. And because they intentionally open up spiritual conversations, they are a great springboard into ongoing Scripture studies. Topical Peace Feast guides can be found at tiny.cc/peace-feast-guides.

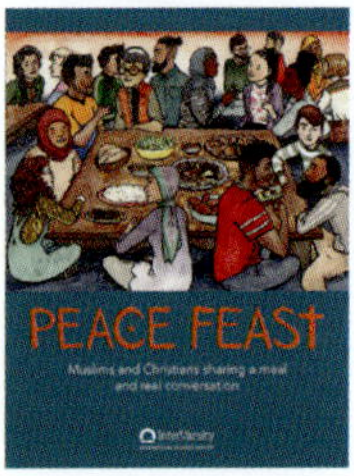

▶ CONCLUSION: THE POWER OF THE WORD

Zohra had been part of a Discovery Bible Study group with several other students for three years. She gradually began to participate more in the discussions by asking questions, praying, and sharing the stories with other Muslims. She would go home each week and video call her mom to tell her the latest story. This was an encouragement to her mother, who had recently become a widow. She would also tell her husband the story she had just learned.

One week, Zohra asked the group to pray for her cousin "He needs to follow Jesus so he can have peace in his life." The group facilitator was surprised and asked, "Well, Zohra, do *you* want to follow Jesus?" Zohra responded, "I think I am very close."

The next morning, Zohra called the group leader and asked if they could meet right away. When the leader arrived at her apartment, Zohra was kneeling on the floor crying and said, "I want to follow Jesus now!" As the leader sat down on the floor to pray with her, Zohra's husband entered the apartment and asked, "What is going on?" The group leader became very nervous and didn't know what would happen. Zohra told her husband that she was praying to trust Jesus. Suddenly, the husband began crying as well and said, "I want to follow him as well. I cannot deal with life on my own. I need God's help, too!"

KEY POINTS

- Invite friends to read the Bible early, often, and let the Word do the work. Our goal is to allow them to meet the real Christ and decide for themselves how to respond.
- Muslims are generally not familiar with our style of inductive study and asking questions about the text, but they catch on quickly.
- Muslims usually enjoy the Bible's lively narrative and hearing longer accounts of familiar characters from the Qur'an.
- Discovery Bible Study is a simple method emphasizing natural communities, discovery—not teaching—and active response.
- Whether reading the Old Testament, New Testament, or even the Qur'an, draw out "gospel threads" that show God's plan of salvation by grace.

ACTION STEP

This week, invite a Muslim friend to read the Bible with you. You could start by sharing a Jesus story or use one of the other ideas at the beginning of this chapter. And if they say yes, start right away!

PRAYER

God thank you for your Word, which is a lamp for my feet and a light on my path (Psalm 119:105). Make me love the Word more and strengthen me to remember Scripture so it can guide me and so I can share it with others. Open a door of opportunity this week to invite a Muslim friend into Bible study. I pray they will know that I do this out of the love I have for them. Open my friend's eyes to understand your truths and respond to Jesus' gracious offer. Thank you for using me to help others find the treasure of your Word. Amen.

6 HELPING FRIENDS BECOME FOLLOWERS

"This is what the kingdom of God is like. A man scatters seed on the ground. Night and day whether he sleeps or gets up, the seed sprouts and grows, though he does not know how. All by itself the soil produces grain—first the stalk, then the head, then the full kernel in the head. As soon as the grain is ripe, he puts the sickle to it, because the harvest has come."

Mark 4:26-29

Spiritual rebirth is a glorious mystery, as Jesus' parable shows. There are multiple characters involved in this story: the man, the seed, the ripened grain, and the soil itself. Each plays different parts. At times the man is engaged, other times waiting and watching, and "he does not know how" the seed sprouts into new life. Growth is credited entirely to the soil, which presumably represents God's presence guiding the process (1 Corinthians 3:5-7). Yet at a later moment, God allows the man to share in bringing in the harvest.

Anyone who has seen a friend come to follow Jesus speaks about the experience with humility. Beware the Christian who talks about "people I've brought to faith." He is misguided at best. As we walk with friends toward Jesus and through faith decisions, we become deeply aware that salvation is the Holy Spirit's glorious, mysterious work.

As we walk alongside friends, we become deeply aware that salvation is the Holy Spirit's glorious, mysterious work.

This chapter discusses the nature of conversion, sharing the gospel in ways Muslims relate to, and helping our friends count the cost of discipleship. Like in Mark 4:26-29 we have parts to play, but it is God who guides the process. Let us learn to wait and watch with much prayer as the Spirit brings growth unto the harvest.

▶ MUSLIMS AND CONVERSION

> Ahmed was involved in an InterVarsity chapter made up of Americans and internationals. Over two years he went from loving the community while hating the God-talk to involvement in Bible studies and receiving prayer. He recognized how good Jesus was for his life and believed he was far more than just a prophet. But though seeking, Ahmed seemed to be stalling out in his journey. His student and staff friends feared he was settling into the "friend zone" and devoted themselves to deep, regular prayer for him. One day Ahmed had a vision of Jesus while in the middle of a lecture. He was shaken up and came to his friends soon after. They spent the evening in listening prayer,[63] and as Ahmed named the fears keeping him from coming to Christ, God sent him a series of visions of Jesus walking alongside him. When one friend said, "Do you think it's time to accept Jesus?" Ahmed tearfully replied, "I just did!"

CONVERSION IS A PROCESS MARKED BY SIGNIFICANT MOMENTS

In the West, we tend to conflate conversion with a moment of decision—usually a raised hand, response card, or sinner's prayer. This reflects the influence of our consumer culture that tries to neatly package and count everything. But theologians describe conversion as a lifelong *process* which includes the *moment* of regeneration, or spiritual rebirth.[64] Some—but not all—of us can recall the moment we surrendered to Jesus, but that moment occurs in the context of a gradual transformation over time.

This gradual pattern fits the experience of many believers from Muslim backgrounds in InterVarsity, who describe coming to faith not as one big step, but countless tiny steps toward Jesus, sometimes over many years. As in Ahmed's story, at each step there were new realizations about who God is, who they are, and how they must respond to his truth. Throughout this chapter, as we describe Muslim friends' transformations, it is understood that the moment of entering Christ's kingdom is part of a process that began earlier and continues into their discipleship.

Many believers from Muslim backgrounds describe coming to faith not as one big step, but countless tiny steps toward Jesus.

THE FIVE THRESHOLDS

InterVarsity's Five Thresholds breaks the conversion process down into distinct stages, or thresholds. It is God who guides a friend's growth, of course, but from experience we have identified key questions and activities that Christians can do to help our friends respond to what the Spirit is doing. Note that this is a model: movement through the thresholds is not linear, and at points people may move backwards, or further from conversion. See appendix A for more.

As you read these, think about your friends. Where are each of them? Are your actions helping them move to the next threshold?

First, a Muslim moves ***from distrust to trusting*** a Christian. Our contribution to help her gain trust is offering friendship through kindness, mutuality (giving and receiving), and service.

Second, a Muslim moves ***from indifference to curiosity***, where she realizes "Your faith isn't what I thought." As we have discussed in previous chapters, most Muslims have a variety or preconceived ideas about Christians and Jesus. When we live winsome, visible faith, she realizes there is more to us than she has been told. International students build

THE FIVE THRESHOLDS

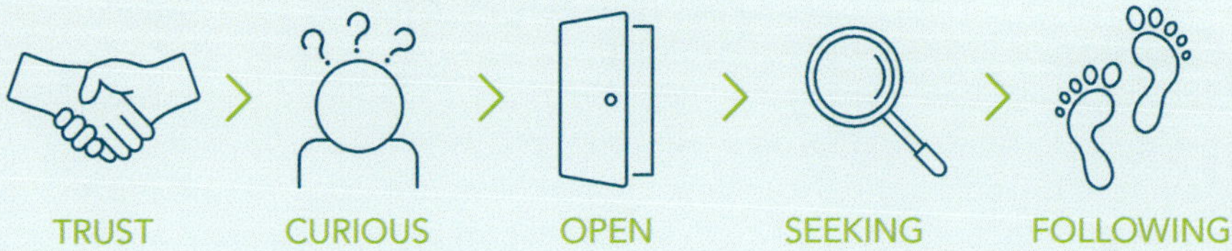

trust and express curiosity quite quickly, but reaching the following thresholds usually takes much more time.

Third, a Muslim moves ***from closed to open to change***. Where previously Jesus was interesting but had little effect on her personal life, at this threshold she experiences the Lord's power and wisdom and recognizes that "Jesus' ways are good for me." This usually involves a step of trusting Jesus in a specific way, like applying the Bible to her life or saying yes to receive prayer.

Fourth, a Muslim moves ***from wandering to seeking***. She recognizes that "Jesus may be the true way" and begins to own the journey and pursue him actively. We help this transition by engaging her questions intelligently and clarifying the gospel message. Muslims may move back to threshold 3 or 2 as they grapple with the implications of following Christ, and new questions and hesitations arise.

Fifth, a Muslim moves from ***undecided about Jesus to following him*** as Savior and Lord. This is the moment of regeneration, which is sometimes but not always discernible. Loving patience toward our friend at this threshold allows her to prepare her heart, and listening prayer creates space where the Lord himself can minister to her and convince her to cross the line.

It can be helpful to think of a sixth threshold new disciples cross, from ***navigating identity in Christ to missional believer*** ready to take the gospel message to others. This will be covered in chapter 7.

Read the following transformation story and see if you can identify the thresholds.

> Husband and wife Haider and Leila had been warned by others from their conservative South Asian country not to associate with Christians. But soon after they arrived in the US, they joined an English conversation group where they were surprised by the warmth and generosity of their Christian language partners.
>
> They began wondering about these new friends' lives and eventually attended an InterVarsity retreat for international students, even inviting others. Jesus' words about loving your enemies impacted Leila deeply, while Haider struggled with them. Later a different Christian group invited them to a dinner that they did not know was followed by a

group Bible study. The couple was upset and dropped out of Christian community for many months.

Eventually Leila and Haider found their way back to reading the Bible. They wrestled with the divinity of Christ but were deeply drawn to him. Living with a tight-knit Christian family for a brief period gave them an intimate look at faith, and they joined a local church connected to their campus ministry.

Haider and Leila knew that following Jesus would come at a high cost. Prompted by their Christian friends, the couple started to pray for Jesus to reveal himself to them if he is the way. Jesus did, both through the Scripture and in their dreams. When they prayed, entrusting their lives to Christ, the couple felt a weight being removed and God's light shining on them.

▶ SHARING THE GOSPEL

The previous chapters have largely been focused on representing Christ to your friends in the early thresholds. As they progress, share the gospel more clearly and invite them to respond.

BOTH SAYING AND SHOWING

Our witness to Muslim international students includes far more than just words. Jesus used power encounters to validate his ability to forgive sins (Mark 2:1-12). Likewise, our lifestyles and actions in front of Muslims validate the gospel message.

Ayat was proud of her Islamic heritage but also connected to several Christians in an InterVarsity international student chapter. At a retreat she told a Christian student friend she felt "a black hole in my chest every time we read the Bible." The student discerned spiritual warfare and invited Ayat to a time of listening prayer. While in prayer, Ayat had a detailed vision in which she saw Jesus enter a broken-down house. "That's my heart!" she said. Then Jesus restored it by his touch. He then started walking down a beautiful road and invited her to follow. Right then, with the Christian student guiding her, Ayat began following him.

Think of gospel sharing as a deed-and-word combination. Cultures differ in their understanding of the human situation. In chapter 3 we introduced shame and fear, two ways Muslims understand the world and their

relationship with God. The shame-based gospel framework (word) on the next page may connect best with Muslims like Haider and Leila who have experienced the warmth of a loving, genuine Christian community (deed). And the fear-based gospel framework (word) that follows may make sense to someone like Ayat who has felt God's power through prayer, including physical or emotional healing (deed).

WHAT SHOULD WE SAY?

> *"It is almost impossible to cover all the bases of the gospel with a non-believing listener without that person's eyes glazing over. Some parts simply engage her more than others, and, to begin with, a communicator should go with those. Eventually, of course, you have to get to all the aspects of the full gospel in any process of evangelism and discipleship. But you don't have to say everything every time."*[65]
>
> *-Tim Keller*

When we discern an opportunity, how should we explain the gospel to Muslim international students? Following Keller's take, we should highlight parts that connect with each friend's specific felt needs. While there are many additional truths about God to be learned later, we should not get bogged down trying to explain everything at once before inviting our friends to respond.

Time and again, individuals began following Jesus with only a partial understanding of him (Matthew 4:18-22; 9:1-13; Luke 5:1-11; John 4:28-29, 39-42). Fuller comprehension came later in the journey. Many who have walked alongside Muslims into the kingdom observe that once the Holy Spirit is empowering new believers' lives, it becomes easier for them to comprehend additional truths.

What do people need to know to be saved? At the center of the gospel is the truth that Jesus is Savior and Lord. In a broad sense, "Jesus is Savior" means he alone is the one through whom we are reconciled to God. "Jesus is Lord" means he alone is the one we must follow and submit to. This is what we seek to express to our Muslim friends through lifestyle, Bible study, and words.

Below are three frameworks for explaining the gospel. The first two are through the language of shame/honor and fear/power, speaking to ways many Muslims experience the brokenness of the fallen world and our separation from God. The third, tracing the pattern of sacrifice through the message of the prophets, builds on a theme Muslims recognize from Islam.

These are guides to help you see how Muslims might relate to the gospel. They are not rigid scripts, and you do not need to memorize every word. As you read each, see how it expresses the truths that Jesus is Savior and Jesus is Lord. Most people hear the gospel many times before coming to faith in Christ, so do not assume that everything is clear after one conversation. Talk about it often and in different ways.

THE GOSPEL THROUGH THE LENS OF SHAME AND HONOR

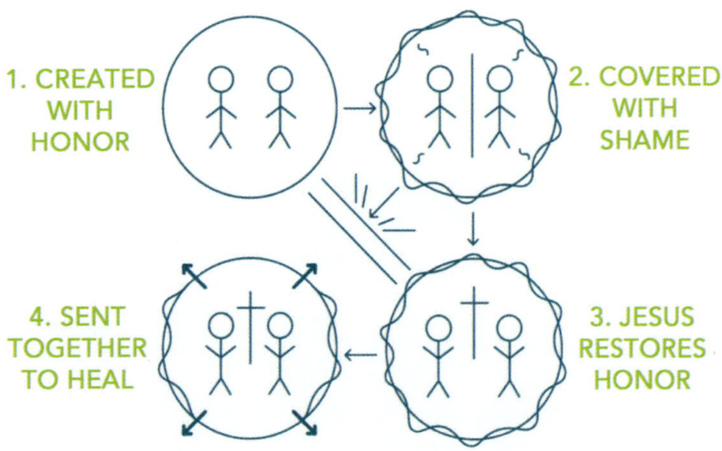

tiny.cc/honorshamegospel | based on InterVarsity's The Big Story

At the center of the gospel is the truth that Jesus is Savior and Lord. This is what we must express to our Muslim friends through lifestyle, Bible study, and words.

There's pain, loss, anger, and suffering everywhere in our world today. But we all long for a better world. And God's Word says that a better world did exist:

1. Like a loving father, God created us as his children. As his family members, we represented his honorable name. People had peace inside themselves and with others, and God honored them by giving them authority to rule and care for the earth. *We were created with honor.*

2. But we rebelled against and broke our relationship with God, dishonoring him and ourselves. Our disloyalty left us exposed to the world and broke our relationships with others as well. We try to save face by making excuses and lying and to cover our shame through pursuing things like careers and possessions. But inside we sense that only a relationship with our Father can heal our shame. *We're covered with shame.*

3. Jesus is our mediator: He lived the perfectly honorable life that we are unable to live, then bore our shame and its full results: abandonment and death. His honorable death to save others broke the power of shame, and his resurrection shows the triumph of God and restores glory to God's name. By turning from our own selfish ways and giving our allegiance to Jesus, we share in his honor. We become members of God's family again and experience internal peace and harmony with others. *Jesus restores honor.*

4. Being restored to God's honorable family, we are freed from the cycle of toxic shame. We go out together in his name and invite all people and all creation to receive God's healing. And God promises that the harmony we begin experiencing now will one day be made perfect and complete. We're sent together to heal.

Note that we can't get to the fourth circle by ourselves, because we cannot remove our own sin and shame. *We need Jesus to be our mediator.*

After you share this, ask your friend, "In which circle do you see yourself and why? In which circle would you like to be?"

THE GOSPEL THROUGH THE LENS OF FEAR AND POWER

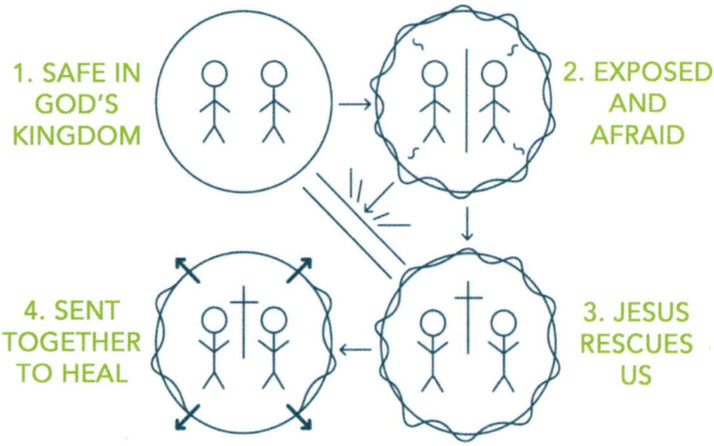

tiny.cc/powerfeargospel | based on InterVarsity's The Big Story

There's pain, loss, anger, and suffering everywhere in our world today. But we all long for a better world. And God's Word says that a better world did exist:

1. God created a good world, with him as its rightful ruler. Living under his protection and power, we could engage the world with confidence. Our first ancestors had peace inside themselves and with others, and God granted us to share in his authority to rule and to care for the earth. *We were safe in God's kingdom.*

2. But we rebelled against God, rejecting his rule and seeking to accumulate power for ourselves. Choosing to live without God's protection, we are exposed to the enemy and his armies of darkness. Fear dominates us. Seeking safety, we hide behind rituals, magic, and curses. But inside we know our deception and that only the righteous power of the true King can heal us. Until then, *we are exposed and afraid.*

3. Jesus is our rescuer: From his throne in heaven, he came to earth to seek and save those he loves. Jesus challenged the enemy, freeing demonized people, healing the sick, and mending broken hearts with the righteous power of God. His death and resurrection broke the hold of fear and death over us. By turning from our own effort and giving our allegiance to King Jesus, we come under his protection. We are now in Christ, and he guards

us in this life and promises that even death cannot separate us. *Jesus rescues us.*

4. Being rescued by Jesus, we no longer need to hide. We go out together with others, spreading the good news of freedom in Jesus' name from fear and death. And God promises that the peace we begin experiencing now will one day be made perfect and complete. *We're sent together to heal.*

Note that we can't get to the fourth circle on our own, because we can never truly save ourselves through false power. We need King Jesus to shield, rescue and rule over us.

After you share this, ask your friend, "In which circle do you see yourself and why? In which circle would you like to be?"

THE GOSPEL AS REVEALED BY ALL THE PROPHETS

> *And beginning with Moses and all the Prophets, he explained to them what was said in all the Scriptures concerning himself.*
>
> *- Luke 24:27*

This is based on InterVarsity's *Shared Prophets: A Qur'an/Bible Discussion Guide*[66] (see appendix D and tiny.cc/shared-prophets-guide).

A student from Southeast Asia studied the common prophets, then asked "Why didn't the people believe Jesus is the Messiah? All the prophets point to him."

The stories of the prophets make clear that God himself provides the means for our salvation, and he does so through *sacrifice.*

When Adam (also called Adam in the Qur'an) and Eve/Hawa sinned, God provided clothing from animal skin to cover their shame, physically and metaphorically.

Noah/Nuh built and boarded the ark, because there was no way to avoid judgment except by obeying the way of salvation that God provided.

God graciously provided a ram as a blood sacrifice for Abraham/Ibrahim and his son. It was by this sacrifice, which died in the son's place, that they were ransomed.

God freed Moses/Musa and the people of Israel from slavery. At Passover, only those who were under the cover of the blood of the lamb were saved because the lamb had already been slain in their place.

The story of David/Dawud shows that even God-honoring prophets sin. No one can attain God's standard of holiness, and like David, we all must confess our sin and ask God to grant us a clean heart.

John the Baptist's/Yahya's ministry was preparing people for the promised Messiah. He confirmed a sign from God, identifying Jesus as the Lamb of God, who takes away the sin of the world.

Finally, Jesus/Isa is the one called the Word of God and Messiah, and is the clear fulfillment of God's way of salvation seen through all the previous prophets. He exercised authority over demons, healed the sick, taught God's way with unparalleled insight, and is the only sinless one, ever. And in an astounding act of love, Jesus became the sacrifice—not

A KEY QUESTION TO DISCERN READINESS

As our friends grow closer to Christ, the simple yet profound question **"Is there anything keeping you from putting your trust in Jesus today?"** helps us discern their readiness. No matter how they respond, you will gain clarity about how to move forward. If your friend is unconvinced about who Jesus is or does not understand the uniqueness of the gospel, continue reading and talking together. If they mistakenly think choosing Christ means wholesale rejection of their culture, correct them lovingly with reassurance that Jesus values them. And if they clearly want Christ but fear the cost of discipleship, go to listening prayer together and ask God for courage to say yes to his invitation.

animal skins, nor their blood, nor a ram, but he himself. His sacrifice fulfilled all earlier ones and was the final and complete answer to sin. And having laid down his life by his own choice, he raised up from the dead in victory!

The message of the prophets is clear: We are deeply broken by sin, and we need God's action to restore us—we cannot do it ourselves. The stories of the prophets point toward Jesus, the perfect sinless lamb, the ultimate sacrifice that redeems (literally saves from, exchanges, or pays for) our sin. We cannot ignore the signs God has given.

After you share this, ask your friend, "Do you see the pattern of God's salvation? Are you willing to receive the sacrifice he has provided, Jesus?"

▶ COUNTING THE COST

> *Then he called the crowd to him along with his disciples and said: "Whoever wants to be my disciple must deny themselves and take up their cross and follow me. For whoever wants to save their life will lose it, but whoever loses their life for me and for the gospel will save it."*
>
> *- Mark 8:34-35*

Many Muslims start the journey toward Jesus eagerly, but around threshold 3 (openness to change) begin to realize the cost of continuing. Suddenly our friend is distant, not returning texts or calls, and hesitating to engage God's truth like he was before. Spiritual attack often ramps up in our friends' lives, either in directly evident ways like nightmares or threats from another person, or unexpected distractions like problems at school or with a distant relative.

Suddenly our friend is distant, not returning texts or calls, and hesitating to engage God's truth like before.

The consequences for Americans coming to faith are almost always vastly different from a Muslim international student's experience. When he puts his faith in Christ, he risks rejection by family and friends, loss of financial help and career options, and even violence or death. Most of us cannot begin to comprehend the weight of this decision.

How do we help our friends who are making these costly decisions? There are three important things we must do when walking alongside someone who is counting the cost of following Jesus: increase prayer, explain what the decision does *not* mean, and offer patient reassurance.

First, now is the time to pray like never before. Gather other believers to pray for spiritual protection and for dreams from Jesus. Plan times for focused listening prayer through his fears and uncertainties. Name the fears, and ask the Holy Spirit to send words, scriptures, or images that show the heart of God.

In chapter 4 we said that many Muslims are having miraculous dreams and visions of Jesus. Supernatural experiences like these have helped many over the final hurdle to accepting Christ. Nabeel Qureshi was a Pakistani American Muslim whose path to faith involved meticulous intellectual study, yet even when his mind was convinced his heart still held back until the Lord sent a series of dreams that led him to Jesus.[67]

Second, make sure your friend knows what choosing Jesus does *not* mean. A Muslim may think that responding to the gospel means he *must* abandon his family and culture. There is a real risk of losing ties, and we cannot sugarcoat the Lord's words in Mark 8:34-35. Jesus commands our whole lives.

But we do not want him saying no because of a misunderstanding of how Jesus, family, and culture mix. Family relationships are treasured in the Bible, as the fifth commandment makes clear. God loves our friend's loved ones more than he can imagine and may use him to eventually carry the gospel to them.

Likewise, following Christ does not mean abandoning all culture and practices from their background. How to assess such practices is as necessary as it is difficult, and we will return to this in chapter 7. Make clear that your friend's journey with Jesus will look different than yours as a western Christian, and that is part of God's good design.

Third, be patient and offer reassurance. If your friend becomes distant while counting the cost, do not read his hesitation the wrong way, as personal rejection of you. Give him time while letting him know you care and are still there for him. Even if he departs your campus or country before committing to Christ, keep in touch and encourage him. Some students have returned home undecided, only to come into the kingdom later in their own country.

When a friend is counting the cost of following Jesus, we must increase prayer, explain what the decision does **not** *mean, and offer patient reassurance.*

Never minimize the struggles your friend is weighing. But if you have faced struggle or persecution in your own walk with Christ, share about it. And show him Jesus' promises in John 14. Our Lord never hides the cost of discipleship. But he gives us his peace as we walk with him.

▶ CONCLUSION

In this chapter we have examined how Muslims are coming to follow Jesus as Savior and Lord, and the part we can play in word and deed. Some new believers' transformations take place quickly; most happen over a period of years marked by many small steps. Whenever it happens, the moment of salvation is beautiful! And it moves us into the adventure of discipleship, which the next chapter focuses on.

KEY POINTS

- Conversion is a gradual process of transformation into Christlikeness, which includes a moment of regeneration.
- The Five Thresholds describes conversion in distinct stages. You can adopt key practices at each threshold to help your friends respond to the Spirit.
- Asking "Is there anything keeping you from putting your trust in Jesus today?" can help your friend identify barriers to–or readiness for–belief.
- You cannot share every aspect of the gospel at once, but you can highlight parts that connect with each listener's felt needs. These may include restoring honor, protecting from fear, or tracing the message of the prophets.
- When your friend is counting the cost of following Christ, you should increase prayer, explain that trusting Christ does not mean abandoning their family and culture, and offer patient reassurance.

ACTION STEP

Sit with one of the three gospel frameworks highlighted in this chapter until you feel you can explain it comfortably. If you have a friend who is open or seeking, look for an opportunity to share it the next time you are together.

PRAYER

Lord, thank you for the gospel, the good news that Jesus has come offering redemption and hope! I need to keep returning to you to be reminded how good you are and how unique in a world of false hopes. (Take time to reflect on how God saved you, and thank him.)

Holy Spirit, draw my Muslim friends to you. Soften their hearts to see the depth of their sin so that they will be prepared to receive your salvation. Give me your wisdom to discern their readiness, guide my actions and words to share the gospel, and make the message clear to them. Lead my friends into your kingdom, in your timing. In the powerful name of Jesus, Amen.

7 WALKING WITH NEW BELIEVERS

By the time I met Mariam she already had quite the reputation. She was feisty at our events and often would argue loudly about interpretations of the Qur'an, distracting other students. We were always a little relieved when she didn't show up.

So I was amazed when late one night two students called me to say that Mariam had decided to follow Jesus. An experience of answered prayer in Jesus' name led to hours of conversation. Mariam poured out her life story, confessed sin, and said that the God she had been learning about was so good that she was ready to follow him. My students led her in prayer, and we welcomed a new sister into the kingdom.

We had just three weeks to disciple her before the school year ended and Mariam would return home *to* a country where the penalty for choosing Christ is extremely high. We prayed for the Holy Spirit to pour out supernatural understanding of Scripture and that she would grow rapidly. Three of us met with Mariam every day to pray, read, and talk about taking her faith back home. We were in over our heads but bursting with joy and gratitude at the same time.

> In Matthew 19:29, Jesus said, "Everyone who has left houses or brothers or sisters or father or mother or wife or children or fields for my sake will receive a hundred times as much and will inherit eternal life." Sitting with Mariam, I felt the weight of his words like never before.
>
> On the night Mariam was leaving we celebrated, prayed, and made final preparations. I sat with her on the couch and talked through the questions she would face back home. Then we drove her to the airport and hugged her goodbye one last time. In the months that followed we kept in touch by texting and encouraged her to keep reading, praying, and pursuing Jesus. One of my students said, "I don't think I will ever forget this." None of us will. Walking with Mariam is one of the greatest privileges of my life, and I will treasure it until we meet again, on this side of eternity or the next.
>
> \- An InterVarsity staff minister

Imagine your excitement if a Muslim friend becomes a follower of Jesus! But what then? How will you walk alongside her? And how will you change, too? For as you journey in discipleship together you both will be transformed by the Spirit.

The word "alongside" is intentional. As someone from a different culture and background, you will not be able to discern every step your friend should take in Christ. Your crucial role is helping her learn to recognize the Spirit's voice speaking in harmony with the Word and to apply it in her life.

This chapter examines how we, as alongsiders, can help new believers practice spiritual disciplines, navigate questions about their identity in Christ and how to share it with others, and address spiritual warfare and persecution.

Alongsiders help disciples recognize the Spirit's voice speaking in harmony with the Word and apply it.

▶ CLOSE DISCIPLESHIP IN A GRACIOUS ENVIRONMENT

Discipleship is not a one-hour-a-week job. Your friend will benefit from seeing all aspects of your life. This may seem daunting but is manageable with creativity. Bring him with you to run errands. Invite him into your home to be around your roommates or family or even to stay in your home for a while. Perhaps he is already connected to a Christian group or local church. Still, consider carefully if he is being well cared for because most Christians have no idea how to disciple believers from Muslim backgrounds.

Discipleship is not a one-hour-a-week job. Your friend will benefit from seeing all aspects of your life.

> Abaz received Christ joyfully but within a month was pushing back against Dev's ideas. "Growing up, my religion was all about rules and regulations. At first I felt free in Jesus, but now it seems you're dropping a whole lot of new rules on me!"

Discipleship must happen in an environment of grace. Islam is heavy on directives, and this is how most Muslims grow up relating to God. For Abaz, a loving Christian community and powerful times in prayer were central in coming to faith in Christ. He felt dissonance when Dev started giving discipleship "assignments."

This highlights a common problem. We want our friends to grow in a variety of areas, and in our effort to get there we push too much, too fast. To the new believer it feels like we began by the Spirit but are continuing by the flesh (Galatians 3:3).

Keep grace central in how you talk about God and also in the rhythms of discipleship. A good rule of thumb for the first steps immediately after coming to Christ is to keep doing the same things that got your friend there. If prayer was central to her journey toward Jesus, keep praying together often and deepen those times. If you were already reading the Bible together, you might continue in the exact same book.

Within the context of a close relationship in a gracious environment, here are some focus areas for walking alongside new disciples.

KINGDOM COMMUNITY

Every believer needs to be in community, but not all groups are equally helpful for believers with Muslim backgrounds. In chapter 5, we observed that Christianity in the US is indelibly shaped by American culture.

The large events, expensive sound systems, revealing clothing, and individualistic self-expression at our gatherings are extremely different from the house churches most of our friends will join back home. Indoctrinating them to our style now will make reentry harder.

The best kingdom community for our friends is a house church or small group where members are deeply connected and practice simple worship, prayer, and Bible study. Aim for this, but if they are involved in an American church, then make clear that Jesus' church comes in diverse forms around the world.

In their enthusiasm, Christian communities often "platform" new believers from Muslim backgrounds by asking them to share their testimonies in front of large crowds and heaping praise on them for the heroism of following Jesus. This is damaging to discipleship in several ways. First, slavish adoration puffs up, centralizing them in the story rather than Christ. Second, public speaking pushes the speaker to draw sharp lines around topics that they are still working out—about Islam, their family, and their identity and plans for the future. Finally, these testimonies have a habit of ending up on the internet with photos, videos, and names attached. Celebrate your friend's salvation! But do so privately and humbly to protect them.

SOAK IN THE BIBLE

You cannot spend too much time in the Word! If you haven't already, get your friend a Bible in their native language. Study individual passages deeply and also skim lengthier portions to learn the big picture of God's story ("Read John 1-12 this week, noting your questions and thoughts.")

As you read, continue to draw out the gospel and its implications for everyday life. Most Muslims default to a works-centered worldview ("I obey, therefore I am accepted") so a gospel-centered worldview ("I am accepted, therefore I obey")[68] is wonderful, yet unfamiliar. Thank Jesus that he has already fulfilled what is required and then respond to that text in joyful gratitude. A key question to continually ask is "What would (or should) this look like in your home country?"

Following Jesus Together (tiny.cc/following-jesus-together) is InterVarsity's discipleship guide designed specifically with Muslim international students in mind. It is built on the Discovery Bible Study format, with minimalist styling to aid cultural translatability. In thirteen chapters it covers crucial topics such as the fatherhood of God, Jesus as Lord and Savior, spiritual disciplines, sharing faith, and persecution.

Practice **discovery** *over* **teaching** *so new believers learn to seek God themselves, directly, rather than treating you as a go-between.*

Practice *discovery* over *teaching* so new believers learn to seek God themselves, directly, rather than treating you as a go-between. When your friend asks a question, turn to a Bible passage that speaks to that issue and discuss how it applies. When asked about an aspect of your lifestyle, tell about not just your actions but the biblical principles that back them up.

NAVIGATING IDENTITY

In the last chapter we introduced the Five Thresholds of conversion, and hinted at a sixth, moving from navigating identity to missional believer. Brand new disciples are still working out their identity as believers ("Am I now a Christian, a Muslim, a follower of *Isa*, or something else?") and sorting out their theology ("How does the Trinity work?") This is deep transformation, and it often plays out over years. It took early Christians several hundred years to hammer out a definition of the Trinity—and if asked, you might describe it incorrectly right now! Fortunately, our status before God is based on Christ's faithfulness, not our own understanding. Be patient, help him keep reading, praying, and listening to God, and trust the Spirit to do the work over time.

As a new believer grows in Christ, questions about old traditions will come up. What should she do about fasting during Ramadan, praying at fixed times of day, eating pork, or wearing a hijab? How should she regard Muhammad? If your friend simply rejects everything in her past, she overlooks the good in her culture and distances herself from loved ones. This has led many to loneliness and eventually walking away from faith. On the other hand, if she uncritically accepts everything in her past, she denies the uniqueness of the gospel and the real change that has taken place in her. But who are you, as a cultural outsider with limited understanding, to make these judgment calls? What should you do?

Neither rejecting nor accepting everything from a disciple's past is healthy.

Critical contextualization[69] is a process to answer these types of questions. Ideally this takes place in a community of new believers from the same culture. Among international students this is rarely possible, but a sensitive alongsider can help an individual through the process.

There are three steps in critical contextualization. First, the new believer deeply studies the meaning of the tradition. "What exactly do we mean when we fast during Ramadan?" Second, she studies the Bible. "What does God's Word say about fasting?" Some traditions are not addressed directly, but she may find analogous examples. Finally, she prayerfully evaluates if the tradition can be *retained* as is, must be *rejected* as incompatible with life in Christ, or can be *reinterpreted* with new, biblical meaning.

Believers with Muslim backgrounds must make well thought-out choices to retain, reject, or reinterpret, and disciples around the world will reach different conclusions, fitting with 1 Corinthians 8:1-13. The Lord may even lead them to change their choices at different stages of spiritual growth.

CRITICAL CONTEXTUALIZATION

Adapted from Paul Hiebert

"WHAT SHOULD WE DO ABOUT OUR OLD WAYS?"

- Prayer posture
- Traditional holidays
- Music
- Fasting
- Visiting the mosque
- Wearing head coverings
- Saying Shahada
- Visiting healers

"OLD IS 100% BAD"
BLANKET REJECTION

- Old ways continue secretly to meet felt needs: conflicted faith
- Family and community reject the gospel as foreign
- Extraction, no witness
- Syncretized faith—does not fit believer's native culture

"OLD IS 100% GOOD"
UNCRITICAL ACCEPTANCE

- New ways not embraced: stunted discipleship and growth
- Family and community do not see change
- Blending in, no witness
- Syncretized faith—does not fit believer's new life in Christ

EVALUATE: CRITICAL CONTEXTUALIZATION

1. Analyze personal and social meaning of the old way
2. Study Scripture for relevant passages
3. Evaluate: **retain**, **reject**, or **reinterpret** old ways

One day, soon after she became a believer, Hafsa noticed that the soles of her slippers were facing up as they sat on the floor. She quickly jumped off the bed to turn them sole-side down, because in her culture it is *haram*, forbidden, to have something dirty facing a person. Then she stopped, telling herself, "Jesus doesn't care if the shoes are facing up. What matters is that we are clean on the inside." Hafsa has since grown into a mature follower of Christ and made many conscientious decisions about her traditions. She maintains cultural norms of care for her family and elders. She continues praying five times a day and fasting, but both with a focus on Jesus. Hafsa says that any practice that does not contradict the Lord's teachings should be retained, particularly by believers living in very conservative communities.

ENGAGE SPIRITUAL WARFARE

I was out to dinner when my phone rang, but when I saw that it was Katia I answered right away. She and a friend were discipling a brand-new believer, Aisha, and we were speaking nearly every day. "Umm, Aisha is on the floor clutching her stomach! We were praying after studying a passage and then she just fell over. What do we do?"

Spiritual warfare is common in early discipleship. In Ephesians 6:11-17, Paul exhorts readers to put on the full armor of God to take a stand not against

QUESTIONS AN ALONGSIDER SHOULD REFLECT ON

1. GENERAL: What have ___ and I done together and discussed lately? What questions is ___ asking lately?
2. GOSPEL: How does/would ___ understand and express the gospel message?
3. SPIRIT: Where do I see evidence of the Holy Spirit working in ___'s life?
4. PRAYER: How is their prayer life? Is ___ comfortable praying aloud? Alone?
5. WORD: What is ___ reading in the Bible lately? Is he reading and memorizing in his heart language? Is he obeying what he learns?
6. WITNESS: Who is ___ sharing his faith in Jesus with?
7. COMMUNITY: Where does ___ have kingdom community with other believers? Who else is involved in his discipleship?
8. CULTURE: In what ways is ___ retaining his unique cultural identity? How can I encourage this?
9. CONCERNS: What areas of ___'s life are concerning? Are there areas where discipleship seems to be stalling out?
10. DECISIONS: What lies ahead for ___? (Baptism, telling family, witnessing, reentry…)
11. CHANGES: What one or two changes in my investment in ___ right now would be of greatest help?

flesh and blood, but against spiritual forces of evil. The Holy Spirit resides in all believers, but we are still susceptible to spiritual attack.[70] In verse 18 Paul adds, "And pray in the Spirit on all occasions with all kinds of prayers and requests." In moments of attack pray, worship and praise God, and quote Scripture. Katia and her friend laid hands on their new sister and prayed, and as Aisha joined them in worshiping God the pain gradually released.

In chapter 4 we said that new believers' growth can be hindered by sins and wounds from their past. These give the enemy a foothold to attack, like rats feeding on garbage.[71] This is exactly what happened with Yunus. While visiting a Muslim-majority country I met this young man, a new believer, who was suffering splitting headaches and hearing voices. "As soon as you entered the room," he said to me, "a voice started telling me 'Get out of this place, you don't want to be here!'" The next day Yunus, his Christian friend, and I spent more than an hour in prayer as he renounced a variety of rituals from his past. As we prayed about a specific curse, the headaches and voices came back, and I felt palpable heaviness in the room. But as Yunus cried out to Jesus, the darkness lifted. Calling on Jesus' name is powerful (Acts 3:6,16; Luke 10:17; tiny.cc/cleansingprayer).

PREPARE FOR PERSECUTION

> *Dear friends, do not be surprised at the fiery ordeal that has come on you to test you, as though something strange were happening to you. But rejoice inasmuch as you participate in the sufferings of Christ, so that you may be overjoyed when his glory is revealed.*
>
> *- 1 Peter 4:12-13*

Throughout this handbook we have sought to describe Islam and Muslims with deep love and respect. Our Christian witness does not require that we denigrate other religions. Rather, we openly point to Jesus the Messiah as the way, the truth, and life for all, trusting God to do his work in hearts.

But there is no getting around the painful fact that most of the world's Muslim cultures do not tolerate conversion to Christ. This is easily demonstrated by Open Doors' World Watch List, where Islam is the dominant religion in an astonishing 38 of the top 50 countries "where Christians suffer very high or extreme levels of persecution and discrimination for their faith."[72] Muslim international students who come to follow Jesus, and indeed the majority of the world's believers outside the West, are likely to face persecution in their lifetimes.

Ripken describes three types of persecution: from the state, from ideological (religious) institutions, and from family and society, which is the worst type.[73] The US receives internationals from countries where each of these types of persecution exist.

In many nations, a son or daughter now following Jesus is perceived to have brought shame on the family which must be purged. One new believer, while back in his home country, received a call from his brother who threatened his life but gave him twenty-four hours to leave first. That warning seems to have been intended as an act of mercy. Many other families are fine with their child following Jesus provided they keep quiet about it. This is, of course, not a long-term solution.

Challenges come in other forms, too. Believers from Muslim backgrounds face difficulties finding a spouse, navigating job markets, and attending cultural events. In countries with both Christian and Muslim communities, churches—many of which face their own persecution—may distrust and be legally barred from welcoming believers from Muslim backgrounds. Even as we celebrate new life in Christ, alongsiders must lament the lonely road that many walk.

Prepare for persecution by talking about it ahead of time while helping the new believer develop a deep, sustaining relationship with the Lord. Much of mainstream Western Christianity is built on avoiding discomfort and practicing relatively easy faith. But the actual text of the New Testament stuns us out of such complacency. "Everyone who wants to live a godly life in Christ Jesus will be persecuted" (2 Timothy 3:12), because they persecuted our Lord and "a servant is not greater than his master" (John 15:20).

Prepare for persecution by talking about it ahead of time while simultaneously developing a deep, sustaining relationship with the Lord.

Paul lost all things, but gladly traded them for "the surpassing worth of knowing Christ Jesus my Lord" (Philippians 3:8) from whose love nothing can separate us (Romans 8:38-39). With your friend, drink deeply from God's promises to be with us through persecution and loss, and cling to the hope of glory that outweighs earthly struggles.

SHARING FAITH, AND BAPTISM

> *"At every significant turn in a disciple's journey, they need to address two questions: 'How can my witness be preserved as best as possible within my community?' and 'How can I live as a reproducible model?'"*[74]
>
> *- Martin Accad*

It is healthy for a growing disciple to want to share Jesus with his loved ones and to make a public declaration of faith through baptism. Yet nothing triggers angry reactions from the Muslim community like these two moves. It is not our job as alongsiders to tell a disciple what to decide. Our role is to help him recognize and obey God's voice and do so wisely.

In general, it is wise to witness by living good news before speaking good news (1 John 3:18). The new believer should act so that family will notice

AHMED'S JOURNEY

Six months after he came to Christ I spend time with Ahmed, whose story we read in chapter 6. He shared vulnerably over the course of our two-hour conversation, and his discipleship journey displays themes common to many others.

MIRACULOUS CALLING

In the weeks leading up to his decision, Ahmed had a series of visions of the Lord that nudged him over his final barriers to belief. In one he saw himself during "meaningful moments, good and bad, from my life, and through all of them Jesus was there with me." He was overcome in retelling this to me, saying "That was just the work of the Spirit. He moves wonderfully." Now as a disciple of Christ, these visions were bedrock giving Ahmed confidence in his new faith.

DISCIPLESHIP IN STOPS AND STARTS

The alongsiders in Ahmed's life were eager to invest in their friend's growth. But Ahmed, who by his own admission was not the most focused student, took a more leisurely route. At times he grew frustrated with a discipleship "plan" that he felt was burdensome. He could be hard to contact. His friends wanted quicker change but tried to be patient.

NAVIGATING IDENTITY

Ahmed claimed the title Christian but still respected his culture and some of the stories he was raised in. "They're my heritage,"he said. He knew he's deeply different from before and was navigating what exactly that meant. I was encouraged by his sifting. Though he was living within fuzzy boundaries, he was increasingly centered on Jesus and his gospel. Our conversation was peppered with references to Scripture he was engaging and what he was praying about.

QUESTIONS ABOUT THE FUTURE

Ahmed's family did not yet know of his faith in Christ. He believed they would have him killed immediately. He recognized that God calls people into risky obedience, and rhetorically asked, "Am I supposed to go back there and publicly declare myself? Because certain death doesn't seem right. But maybe I will go back, someday." I said to him, "I can't make that decision for you, and I believe the most important thing right now is to deepen your roots in God. We aren't required to know how to obey in 50 years, but rather to obey what we know, today." I shared a prayer taught to me long ago: "Each day ask 'Lord, am I as surrendered to you as I know how to be, right now?' and suggested that if he prays that, God will reveal his next step.

positive changes, seeing that he is becoming a better son or brother. He can serve and be more helpful around the house or write a letter to his parents from school expressing appreciation for their sacrifices so he could study. If others see all this first, it may be easier when they learn that Jesus is the reason.

Consider who to share with first. Is there one friend or family member who is gentle, trustworthy, and more open to new ideas? Start there. Help your friend prepare for these conversations. Encourage him to reflect on his journey to Christ and the many small turning points that helped him move from closed to open. Discuss how he can emphasize continuity: how his faith upbringing helped him desire a life that honors God, which he is now pursuing wholeheartedly.

In general, it is wise to witness by living good news before speaking good news.

Similarly, the when and how of baptism deserves prayerful consideration. Baptism is a biblical command, but it is also the point where many new believers are cut off.[75] This is especially true when the baptism is done at the hands of Westerners. At times we have asked believers with Muslim backgrounds in the US to baptize new disciples. If you cannot arrange this, consider waiting until your friend returns to his home country to be baptized there.

A related difficulty concerns money. If he is financially dependent on his parents, your friend will need help if he is cut off when they learn of his new faith. Believing friends may need to mobilize with housing and financial support. Certainly this is the time to be the family of God. Yet money issues are complicated. Be careful about mixing faith and finances in a way that creates ongoing dependency, which has confused and mixed the motives of many new believers.

▶ CONCLUSION

Walking alongside new believers with Muslim backgrounds is a deep privilege and worth our best effort. As we help them learn to hear and respond to Christ's guidance, we, too, mature in our faith. Our prayer is that international students will be formed into the image of Jesus while also uniquely reflecting the culture they come from. This will prepare them to transition back to their home country, which is the subject of the next chapter.

KEY POINTS

- Alongsiders help disciples hear the Spirit's voice and apply it in their lives.
- Discipleship is not a one-hour-a-week job, so look for ways to invite your friend into your life.
- The best kingdom community is a house church or small group where members are deeply connected and practice simple worship, prayer, and Bible study.
- New believers are still navigating their identity and theology, so walk beside them patiently.
- Using critical contextualization, your friend may decide to retain, reject, or reinterpret old practices.
- Expect spiritual warfare and persecution and dig deep into God's Word and promises.

ACTION STEP

Use critical contextualization, introduced in this chapter, to evaluate some of your own faith practices—not necessarily to be rejected, but to note the difference between biblical essentials and cultural diversity. Some examples include bowing your head in prayer, singing hymns versus contemporary praise songs, and sitting in rows during church.

PRAYER

God, grant me the privilege of walking alongside a new disciple of Jesus! I want to bless and be blessed, to help shape the faith of another and to have my own faith refined. Help me become the kind of Christian who can serve in this role: generous with my time, welcoming others into my life, living an example worth imitating, centered on your Word, and knowing the voice of your Spirit. Strengthen me to endure whatever persecutions, large or small, will come into my own life. You gave your all for me, and you are worth my very best, Jesus. Amen.

8 PREPARING FOR REENTRY

"Yours may be the most strategic ministry in the world."

Years ago, a senior leader in the Middle East spoke those words to a group of InterVarsity staff. He had just learned about international student ministry and was blown away by our access to Muslims from every corner in the world, our freedom to openly engage spiritual topics together, and the potential of internationals returning as Christ-followers who could shape their own countries' spiritual futures.

I remain deeply humbled by this veteran's words, but in addition to motivating me, they haunt me because I fear we are not living up to our potential.

This leader correctly named the dream: that international student returnees who meet Jesus here will reintegrate back home and continue growing in faith (*this* is successful reentry) so that they can become, like the woman at the well in John 4, gospel witnesses to their families and communities. Oh, how we long to see this dream realized!

The dream is that international student returnees who meet Jesus here will reintegrate back home, continue growing in faith, and become witnesses to their communities.

But good reentry is hard. Muslim international students face a variety of challenges in transitioning back home. And we, their American friends, face our own challenges in understanding their world and offering support. In this chapter we will describe the journey ahead of our friends and sketch a road map for helping them prepare while they are still with us.

▶ CHALLENGES AWAITING RETURNEES

In general, Muslim international students return to contexts vastly different than the West. As with all international students, they have grown and changed from their experience abroad. They are saying goodbye (at least physically) to friends. Many internationals have been part of Christian ministries where they felt welcomed, were deeply connected, and held roles serving other students. In the months after return, joy about being reunited with families is mixed with reverse culture shock.[76]

There are additional challenges specific to Muslims who are seeking or have met Jesus while abroad. Holidays, calendars, and social gatherings in Muslim-majority communities are oriented around practicing Islam. Jesus-followers walk a tightrope of decisions and often feel deep loneliness. In contrast to the independence they had in the US, decisions back home may have been made for them. Jobs may already be lined up in family businesses and marriages arranged. Returnees, particularly women, may have little authority over what they do and where they go that will affect their freedom to grow spiritually. One sister, back home in an extremely conservative region, could not even read her phone's Bible app because her parents knew the phone password and checked it often.

Once I had the chance to visit Omar, a new believer, in his home county. Omar was under the microscope both at home and work, and the only time he was alone was during his commute. He had no fellowship with Christians, and I could tell he was struggling under the pressure. We spent the day talking, praying, and reading the Bible. We cried together, and I told him, "You are not alone. There are others like you in this city and around the world." I wish I could say that Omar is thriving today, but I do not know if he ever found community or if he is still following Jesus.

Eid festival in India

▶ THINK REENTRY FROM THE START

Every aspect of ministry with Muslim international students should be done knowing that they are only passing through our country. This simple truth is hard to hold in mind when you have only known someone here, on your campus in America. They come from a different culture and part of the world, are here for a few short years, and will return there to live the rest of their lives.

"But don't many stay here after graduating?" you may be wondering. It is true that many internationals *want* to stay in the West, and a portion of them will succeed through postdocs or jobs and build lives here. But we do not know the plans the Lord has for our lives. Many who intend to stay end up returning later. It is our obligation to help them develop biblical faith that fits their culture. This is how they will be able to reach their families and communities. Even those who stay in the US maintain lifelong connections back home and can be salt and light through those relationships.

Think reentry from the start. Everything in this handbook has been written from this perspective. This is why we honor the cultures of Muslims we meet, asking about them and learning about their backgrounds. This is why we include the question "How would you live this out in your home country?" when reading Scripture together. This is why we learn to share the gospel message in ways recognizable as good news to people with different values and desires from our own. And this is why we are sensitive to present diverse images of Christianity and the church befitting our truly global faith.

Every aspect of ministry with Muslim international students should be done knowing that they are only passing through our country.

▶ PREPARE IN THE MONTHS BEFORE DEPARTURE

In the last chapter we met Mariam, who came to faith in Jesus just three weeks before leaving the US to return to her home country. What would you do in this situation? With luck, you will have more time to help your friend prepare. What experiences with the Lord and in community would you want her to have before she departs? How could you help her be ready for the dramatically different context that awaits her back home?

Hopefully you and your disciple friend have been praying about and discussing the return home for a long time. When you are several months from her departure date, it is time to start making specific plans.

Make plans for her spiritual growth and your ongoing investment. How, when, and where will she practice spiritual disciplines, particularly Bible reading and prayer? If a physical Bible is not an option, help her become familiar with an app or website. Following the same reading plan will help you stay connected and make it easier to check in and encourage each other.

Encourage her to memorize verses in her heart language, particularly about God's promises. Scripture memorization is a powerful habit, sadly underused in most evangelical circles. The verses you hold in your heart cannot be taken away, and the Spirit has a knack for bringing them to mind to minister to us at just the right time.

Make plans for how the two of you will communicate. Download and start using a secure app like Signal for texting, audio, and video calling. A virtual private network (VPN) protects your internet use and communication from outside spying. At the time of writing, Nord VPN is one of the best paid options, and Proton VPN is a solid free choice. VPNs do not raise suspicion as they are widely used for different reasons around the globe. Try to set up a regular time to continue discipleship together over video call, including setting the time for a first meeting within a few days of her arrival. Depending on your friend's home environment, you may need to establish ground rules for safe communication topics.

It may seem odd, but preparing for specific conversations and questions your friend will face is worthwhile. Friends and family will ask about her time in the US, who she spent time with and what they did, and even detailed questions about the state of her Islamic faith. Answered poorly, these can quickly become uncomfortable or hostile. But if your friend prepares careful responses, these conversations can be the first steps toward eventual witness.

Preparing careful responses to the inevitable questions back home can be the first step toward eventual witness.

Make plans for how she will fellowship with other believers back home. Find out if there is a local church in her city, but remember that in many Muslim-majority countries local churches cannot safely receive believers with Muslim backgrounds. If that is the case, you will need to be more intentional.

If you are part of a church denomination or nationwide campus ministry, you may be connected to Christians in your friend's home country who could receive her for ongoing community and discipleship. Contact these home-country believers as early as possible, and well before your friend's departure. It takes time and trust to prepare these sensitive introductions. If you have no one to contact in her home country and your disciple friend is leaving soon, reach out to us in InterVarsity for help (ism@intervarsity.org).

▶ STAY IN TOUCH

"The campus ministry industrial complex makes it difficult to stay in touch with students once they leave," a colleague remarked with humor and regret. He was referring to the natural flow of our ministry calendars. The default is to say goodbye in June (or December) and shift all focus, relationships, and activities to new students coming in the new semester.

Christians committed to reentry success will have to actively work against this pattern. Granted, you probably will not be so quick to move on from

Muscat, Oman

a friend who came to faith in Christ. But if we are honest, most of us know that staying in touch is difficult in our forward-looking, fast-paced culture.

Kate, a veteran international student minister, travels to visit returnees in their home countries each summer. What a fantastic model for ministry—and for vacation! A visit to your friend back home will be deeply meaningful for both of you and take your relationship with him to a new level. But texting and calling are also meaningful and make it easy to stay in touch anytime.

This is not just for students who have become followers of Jesus, either. For every international who comes to Christ during his time abroad, there are dozens more who are on the journey when their time in the US runs out. They have enjoyed warm friendships with Christians, had deep discussions about faith, read parts of the Bible, and even experienced God's power in prayer. Keep ministering to them! With threshold 2 (curious) or 3 (open) returnees, keep living your Shema lifestyle through texting. Brandon did this and ended up pastoring Nasir through a dream from Jesus. And give threshold 4 (seeking) returnees a bold encouragement to keep pursuing Christ back home. Silvia continued having Bible studies with her friend Haniya for several years, over video calls.

Bottom line, maintain your relationships. When your new believer friend lands in his home country, you are the strongest faith connection in his life. Read that sentence again and feel the privilege and responsibility. Right at the beginning, try to stay in touch daily. Share verses and prayers to encourage him, and call when possible for deeper conversations. If over the months the frequency of contact goes down as his relationships with local believers grow, this is normal and healthy. Your role will gradually shift from discipler to more of a friend/mentor, but you will have always played a precious role in his life and in God's story for his country.

KEY POINTS

- Successful reentry for ongoing witness is the ultimate goal of international student ministry, so keep it in mind at every stage of your relationships.
- Returnee believers from Muslim backgrounds face all the "normal" challenges of international students going home, plus limitations on how they can practice their faith.
- In the months before departure, prepare plans for how they will spend time with Jesus, communicate with you safely, and connect with local believers.
- Stay in touch with returnees through visits, texting, and video calls, so your ministry can continue.

ACTION STEP

Read chapter 13: "Vision for the Journey," and topic K: "Reentry" in *Following Jesus Together*, (tiny.cc/following-jesus-together). Envision what it would be like to read this as a new believer international student preparing to move home after years in the West. Spend time praying for returnees.

PRAYER

Sovereign God, you rule over all the peoples and nations of the world, and one day every knee will bow and every tongue confess that Jesus Christ is Lord (Philippians 2:10-11). But on this side of that glorious day, many former international students who have returned home live under daily pressure and persecution for following you, Jesus. Sustain their faith with steadfastness and peace that passes understanding. Guide them to witness creatively, that whole families and communities would come to trust the Messiah.

Father, strengthen international student ministries, that we would improve at reentry. Give us a deeper understanding of this work. Teach us perseverance to walk alongside returnees faithfully. And strengthen the partnerships of believers around the globe to work well together, that returnees will find community and you will be glorified by your global church. Amen.

9 PLANNING FOR THE CAMPUS

As you complete this handbook, we pray that you feel motivated and equipped to connect with Muslim international students! You may be brand new and just getting started in this ministry. Or you may already have one or more Muslim friends and would like to be more intentional and invite other Christians along. You could be asking these kinds of questions about your next steps:

- Who's with me?
- How do we prepare?
- Where should we start?
- What are the best activities?

This concluding chapter will help you answer those questions and make specific plans for your campus, drawing from the Apostle Paul's ministry, and particularly his approach in the city of Athens. Before going further, read Acts 17:16-34.

WHO'S WITH ME?

"While Paul was waiting for them in Athens..." Acts 17:16

Paul worked in ministry teams. In verse 16 he was waiting for Silas and Timothy (see v.15) to arrive and join him. At other times Paul served alongside Barnabas and John Mark (Acts 13:2-5), Priscilla and Aquila (Acts 18), Titus (Galatians 2:1-10), and others (Acts 19:22, 29; 20:4). These friends traveled with him, joined him in proclaiming the gospel and shepherding house churches, prayed for him, and suffered alongside him.

Central in InterVarsity's mission is building witnessing *communities*. We value ministry in teams. We encourage you to gather others to join you in building relationships with Muslims. Think about the people in your small group or other Christians you know from your school or church. Who is passionate about spending time with people, sharing Jesus, and exploring cultures? Who is deeply committed to prayer, even behind the scenes as an intercessor?

Find those people and share your testimony of being blessed through friendships with Muslims. Or better yet just bring another Christian along when you hang out with your Muslim friends! They will see the warm hospitality and vibrant, faith-sharpening discussion and get hooked. That's how many of us began. As your group becomes a team, remember the sensitive gender dynamics between women and men in most Muslim cultures.

If you are not a student, reach out to the campus ministry at your local school to see if there are opportunities for you to volunteer with international student ministry. Volunteers are a huge part of InterVarsity's work all across the country, and we would be glad to welcome you.

Take a moment now to write down the names of Christians who might be good partners in connecting with Muslim international students. Reach out to them this week.

HOW DO WE PREPARE?

PRAYER

Paul prayed. I mean, the guy *prayed*. His letters are filled with examples of how he prayed: for the growth of those he served (Romans 1:8-10, 15:5-6, 1 Corinthians 1:4-9, Ephesians 3:14-21, Philippians 1:3-6), that God would go before him and open people's hearts (Romans 10:1, Ephesians 6:19-20, Colossians 4:2-4), asking others to intercede for him (Romans 15:30-33), and abundantly praising God (Romans 11:33-36, 2 Corinthians 1:3-7, 2:14-16, Ephesians 1). True, prayer is not directly mentioned in Acts 17:16-34, but what do you think he was doing while walking around the city, looking carefully at the Athenians' idols?

Whatever your prayer life looks like now, start by increasing it just a bit.

Likewise, we must develop a lifestyle of prayer to thrive in ministry among Muslim international students. Prayer connects our hearts and will to the Father's, that we will love like he does and do what he would have us do.

Whatever your prayer life looks like now, start by increasing it just a bit. Pray by name for Muslim-majority countries that send international students (see several on page 37)—that doors will remain open for students to come and justice will reign in these nations. With your Christian friends, pray for the plans you are making and for each other, laying on hands and asking the Spirit to fill you up. When you meet a Muslim on campus, pray for them as you walk home later. And in conversations, try to grow the habit of listening for the Lord and how he might be directing you—while still paying attention to your friend!

LEARNING

Paul had been deeply schooled in the Jewish religious tradition for much of his life. This equipped him well for ministry with his fellow Jews, but the Greek philosophy in Athens was quite different. So Paul the teacher became Paul the learner. While waiting for his friends to arrive he spent time walking through the city (17:23). Paul was inductively studying the culture of the people he wanted to share Jesus with.

You do not need to know everything about Muslims before getting started.

But while we strongly encourage you to prepare yourself to engage intelligently and sensitively, do not be overwhelmed by all there is to learn! You do not need to master everything about Muslim-Christian history, Islamic beliefs, or Bible study before getting started. (Spoiler alert: you will never master these topics.)

If you and your Christian friends are eager to jump in, for now just read some of the cultural and ministry tips in chapters 3 and 4. You can continue reading the other chapters along the way. And ask your Muslim friends to be your teachers and tell you about their cultures and faith. They will educate you in ways no handbook can.

Take a moment now and make a commitment to increase your prayer life, in one concrete way. Then, if you have not already, read chapters 3 and 4 this week.

▶ WHERE SHOULD WE START?

Study Paul's journeys and you will see that he traveled with a mixture of planning and flexibility. His ambition was to preach the gospel where Christ was not known (Romans 15:20), so he aimed for new places and audiences. He considered the locations of the people he was connected with and thought ahead about where he wanted to go (Romans 15:23-25). Yet he also listened to the Holy Spirit when one door closed and another opened (Acts 16:6-10).

Network mapping is a simple activity to help you and your friends recognize where God may already have provided an open door. Talk together about the places and people you are connected to. Consider your dorm or neighborhood, international student organizations or ethnic student clubs, and other social groups and networks. Write the names of Muslims you know in these places and note also what people and groups they are connected to. Often after this exercise it is easy to see where you should start spending your time.

Like Paul, make a plan but be flexible. This is a lost art in most of our lives as we stack our schedules so full that we lack margin. Being too busy makes it hard to hear the Holy Spirit's whisper. Recall that most Muslim cultures are oriented more around relationships than time. As you follow your networks there will be chances to meet friends of your friends. If you choose relationships over rushing, you can easily add new friends.

NETWORK MAP EXAMPLE

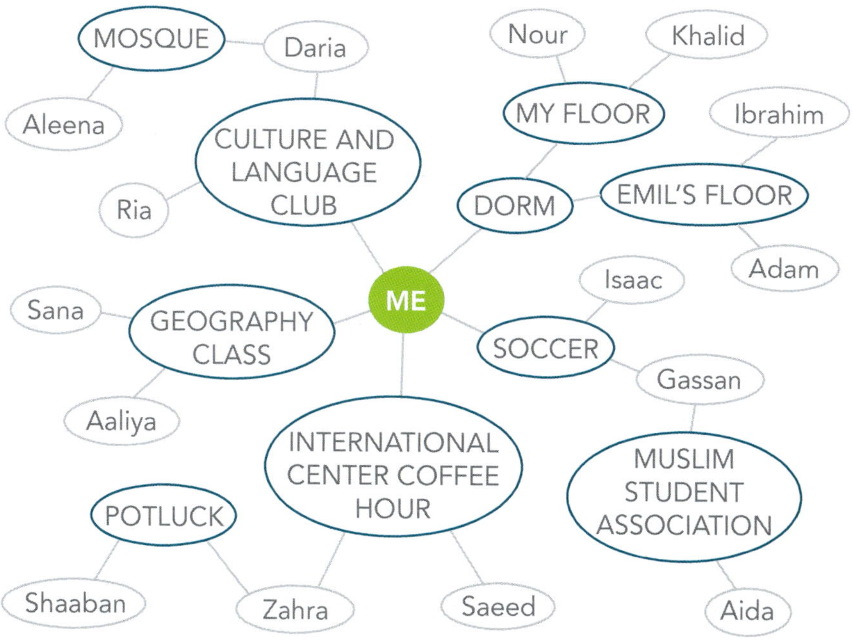

Take a moment now to create a network map. When you're together with your Christian friends, combine all your maps together.

▶ WHAT ARE THE BEST ACTIVITIES?

Paul sought out spiritual conversations in the marketplace and synagogue (17:16-17). This led to an invitation to speak on the Areopagus, a broad, flat-topped rock that served as a meeting place for scholars to discuss the latest ideas (17:19). From there he preached his evangelistic message. After that, some dismissed his message, but others wanted to learn more and eventually became disciples of Jesus (17:22-34). There was a natural focusing effect: Paul started broad, conversing with anyone, but over time some drifted away while the most interested ones remained.

Start with broad activities where you go out among Muslim internationals and build new connections, usually in group settings. These could include:

- Picking students up at the airport when they arrive in the US
- Serving as English language partners
- Visiting Muslim neighbors
- Playing soccer on campus (Watching a televised match in a dorm lounge is a great choice, too!)
- Stopping by a mosque or Islamic center around noon on Fridays (ask first)

- Attending a campus club for international students or a certain ethnic group (ask first)
- Prayer walking campus and starting conversations

From there, it is natural to invite your new friends to more personal venues where you can get to know each other more deeply. These could include:

- Sharing a meal, coffee, or tea—these are where friends meet in most Muslim cultures!
- Hiking, or visiting local parks or landmarks
- Planning a Peace Feast (see appendix B)

In these settings we build genuine friendships while also living our Shema lifestyle (chapter 4), a commitment to show our faith openly in a warm, non-threatening manner. Ask spiritual questions and make spiritual statements. You may see opportunities to connect Jesus stories to your conversations.

In smaller settings we can have richer spiritual conversations and invite Muslim friends to read Scripture together

---

Please do not misunderstand: we are not befriending people only for witness. We seek real, two-way relationships with Muslims whether they express interest in Jesus or not. Living a Shema lifestyle is not about putting on a show, but about being true to who we are—followers of Jesus—and *not editing out* the most core part of our identity. We want and expect the same from our friends! But when we live this way around Muslim international students, a natural consequence is that we attract those who are also genuinely seeking God and open to spiritual conversations.

In smaller settings we can have richer spiritual conversations and invite Muslim friends to read Scripture together (chapter 5). Like Paul experienced after speaking at the Areopagus, some will not be interested in going deeper. This can be painful, but it is part of ministry. There is no need to reject people from friendship because they are not interested in faith. The vast majority of my Muslim friends have not yet opened the Bible with me. But we trust that the Holy Spirit is working the hearts of some people around you, so it is ok to keep looking for them.

Take a moment now to sketch out activities for the next month, from meeting people to building relationships to planning a Peace Feast (tiny.cc/peace-feast-guides).

▶ CONCLUSION: HIGH LOVE, HIGH COURAGE

Christians engaging other religions often lean toward one of two ends of a spectrum, either love or courage. On one side are those who, in their fervor for truth, blast their message in the face of others with little tact or sensitivity. They want to be courageous but come across as unloving. On the other side are those who, in their desire for tolerance, affirm so much about other religions that they lose the uniqueness of Christ. They want to be loving but come across as lacking courage.

In Acts 17, Paul exemplifies both high love and high courage. As always, Paul is crystal clear that his hearers must respond to who Jesus is. There is no alternate path to God than by repenting and trusting the resurrected judge and savior (vs. 29-31). No one went home that day wondering what Paul believed. High courage.

Yet Paul's entire message builds from the culture and beliefs of his audience. After spending time in their city learning about them, his heart was moved. He begins from their belief system (v. 23) and quotes their poets (v. 28), affirming partial truths and their eagerness to know God. High love.

What do you tend toward: high love, high courage, or both?

Where do you lean on the spectrum: toward love at the expense of courage, or courage at the expense of love? Ask the Lord to give you more of the one you need.

In this handbook we have sought to present a high love, high courage approach to ministry among Muslim internationals. We affirm the dignity of Muslims as God's beloved creations. We learn about their cultures in order to affirm their personhood and to communicate relevantly. And with compassion and clarity we offer Jesus, the only Lord and Savior and the greatest gift we can share with those we love. High love, high courage. May you embody both as you connect with Muslim international students.

KEY POINTS

- Gather other Christians to partner with you—people who enjoy people, culture, and sharing Jesus.
- Develop a lifestyle of prayer—it's ok to start small.
- Learn, though you do not need to know everything about Muslims to get started.
- Make plans *and* be flexible to follow new opportunities.
- Start with broad activities to make friends, then find smaller venues where you can have deeper conversations.
- Be open about your faith, and know that some will not be interested, but others will.
- Approach Muslims with both high love and high courage.

PRAYER

Lord, receive the humble offering of my will and guide me in this ministry. Show me Christian friends who share the same heart and help us encourage each other. Teach us to pray! Provide opportunities for us to befriend many Muslim international students and build genuine friendships. Lead us to the ones you are preparing to know Jesus. Release us from thinking we need to have all the answers immediately, but teach us to walk by your Spirit and be ambassadors for Christ. I ask all of this by your power and for the glory of your name, Jesus, Amen.

APPENDIX A THE FIVE THRESHOLDS AND MUSLIM INTERNATIONAL STUDENTS

InterVarsity's Five Thresholds breaks the conversion process down into understandable stages, with practical advice for helping our friends move to faith in Christ.

THE FIVE THRESHOLDS

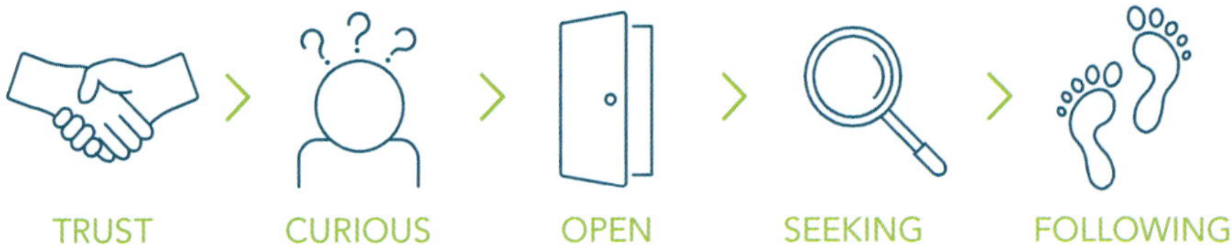

It is God who guides a friend's growth, of course, but from experience we have identified key practices Christians can do to help our friends respond to the Spirit. Note that this is a model: people do not always move steadily upward through the thresholds. At times they may move backwards, to a previous threshold.

▶ THRESHOLD 1: FROM DISTRUST TO TRUSTING A CHRISTIAN

Muslim international students may come to the US never having known a Christian personally and having heard negative stereotypes. Some tell us they were warned to avoid Christians. When you first meet someone, assume they are starting here.

By offering genuine friendship through kindness, service, and mutuality (each person gives and receives), you can build trust. Practice warm hospitality. And do not hide your faith! As you build friendships, being open about your identity as a believer helps build trust with Muslims.

When a Muslim can say, "I know a Christian I trust," she is at the end of this first threshold.

THRESHOLD 2: FROM INDIFFERENT TO CURIOUS

TRUSTING, BUT
INDIFFERENT → VISIBLE FAITH → **CURIOUS**
"YOUR FAITH ISN'T WHAT I THOUGHT."

Muslim friends at the trust threshold enjoy your company and may even come to Christian events, yet still carry general indifference toward our faith. This could be due to a lack of interest in *any* religion, their confidence in Islam, or their preconceptions about Christianity.

Following the SHIPS+ model in chapter 4, live your faith visibly. Share what you are reading and praying about. Ask your friends about their spiritual journeys, and share your own. Include "Jesus in Everyday Conversations" by telling relevant stories of the Messiah. As we display a living faith, our friends begin to be intrigued. See chapter 4 for more.

When a Muslim can say, "Your faith isn't what I thought," he is at the end of this second threshold.

THRESHOLD 3: FROM CLOSED TO OPEN TO CHANGE

CURIOUS, BUT
CLOSED TO CHANGE → EXPERIENCE BIBLE & PRAYER → **OPEN TO CHANGE**
"JESUS' WAYS ARE GOOD FOR ME."

Curious Muslim international students come to events, have spiritual conversations with us, and even study the Bible. But they may still hold Jesus at arms' length because they are not truly open to changing their beliefs. This threshold requires that they take a step towards trusting Jesus in a specific, personal way, which is why crossing it can take a long time.

You can offer opportunities for our friends to discover the goodness of the Lord through experiencing His wisdom and power. As you read the Bible together, encourage specific applications to try out life lived Jesus' way. And offer prayer, that friends might be touched by the Spirit.

When a Muslim can say, "Jesus' ways are good for *me*," she is at the end of this third threshold.

▶ THRESHOLD 4: FROM WANDERING TO SEEKING

Open Muslim international students may read and obey the Bible at times, recognize the uniqueness of Christ, and enjoy Christian prayer. But they are not yet convinced that Jesus is the way, truth, and life. They may be held back by misunderstandings around what exactly the gospel both offers and demands of them, or by other theological and cultural questions.

Now that your friends' hearts have been warmed by the goodness of the Lord, you need to help remove the barriers that stand in the way of belief. Engage their questions intelligently, and clarify the gospel of Jesus as Savior and Lord. Explain the diversity of God's global church and that following Jesus does not require rejecting everything about their culture.

When a Muslim can say, "Jesus may be the true way," he is at the end of this fourth threshold.

▶ THRESHOLD 5: FROM UNDECIDED TO FOLLOWING JESUS

Seeking Muslim friends display clear desire for Jesus but have not surrendered their lives to him. Already since previous thresholds they have begun to recognize the implications of following Christ, but here they count the cost seriously. Some may move back to threshold 3 or 2, closing off in fear or as new questions arise.

Ask the question, "Is anything keeping you from following Jesus, now?" Answers will draw out the remaining barriers. Be patient with your friends as they wrestle with the Lord. Pray deeply for them, and offer listening prayer, asking Jesus to reassure them with words, visions, and dreams that show his love and address their specific fears. See chapter 6 for more.

When a Muslim can say, "Jesus is my Savior and Lord," she is at the end of this fifth threshold. Hallelujah!

In ministry among Muslims, it is helpful to name an additional threshold:

▶ THRESHOLD 6: FROM NAVIGATING IDENTITY TO MISSIONAL BELIEVER

New followers of Christ from Muslim backgrounds love and trust Jesus but are still working out their full identity in Christ. They likely have questions about what to call themselves, what to do about their traditions, and when and how to share their faith with family and friends.

You can help your friends grow into mature, missional believers by walking alongside them in close discipleship within an environment of grace. Help them recognize the Spirit speaking through the Word and make discerning choices about how to live as witnesses to their own communities. See chapter 7 for more.

When a follower of Jesus can say, "I will take the gospel message to others," he is a missional believer.

APPENDIX B PEACE FEASTS

Simple. Real. World-changing.

Peace Feasts bring Muslims and Christians together to share a meal and have deep conversations about the topics we care about most.

peacefeast.net

Peace Feasts are a terrific event to host with your campus group or even just a couple of friends. Imagine a room like the one pictured here. It is filled with both Christian and Muslim students from a variety of countries and backgrounds. As they talk through Peace Feast discussion questions, they are learning about one another's lives, faiths, and scriptures…and enjoying great food!

Peace Feasts are not a typical interfaith event where you hear a formal dialogue between guest lecturers and have little interaction with other participants. Peace Feasts facilitate *heart-level* dialogue by having participants sit together in small groups and share their personal experiences. Some interfaith events promote a watered-down version of "tolerance" by avoiding areas of disagreement. Not Peace Feasts, however, where we encourage sharing about our faiths and comparing areas of similarity and difference, all in a safe and respectful environment.

Peace Feasts are designed to encourage further conversations and deeper friendships between Muslims and Christians. They are also adaptable and scalable. You can host one in your city or on your campus, with anywhere from four to four hundred participants.

Here are some of the questions you will be discussing with your friends:

- Tell us about a person who has played an important role in your faith journey. How did they influence you?
- What is one of your favorite stories from your holy book and why?
- What is it like being a Muslim / Christian in the United States right now? What's something about your faith that is often misrepresented by the media, and that you would like us to understand?

There are also topical Peace Feasts where Muslims and Christians discuss perspectives on subjects such as:

- Justice
- Prayer
- Suffering
- Fasting
- Friendship
- Love
- Hospitality
- Thankfulness
- Jesus

Many people have a series of Peace Feasts throughout the year.

Here is what participants, both Muslim and Christian, are saying about Peace Feasts:
"It's an opportunity to learn our religions' similarities and differences. In that way we can find sisterhood and brotherhood, and peace."
"It was very rewarding! I learned a lot and I found new friends."
"Everyone's asking if we can do this again next month!"
"We've had events like this before, but the Peace Feast was different. The materials gave us a boost and made this the best by far!"

To learn more about hosting a Peace Feast, visit: peacefeast.net

PEACE FEAST

APPENDIX C TURNING OBJECTIONS INTO GOOD CONVERSATIONS

As you connect with Muslim international students, several common objections will come up:

1. The *Injil*, Gospel, has been corrupted.
2. Jesus is not the Son of God.
3. The Trinity does not make sense.
4. Jesus did not die.

Each of these questions arises from what your friends have been taught about Christianity by Islamic traditions. Before responding, consider intent, heart, and tone.

First, consider their intent. As we discussed in chapter 5, Muslims at the trust and curiosity threshold often–though not always–ask questions to test you, and even to provoke a debate. They may not be interested in hearing an answer, so it might be best to detour the conversation until a later time. But Muslims at the open and seeking thresholds, who are already drawn to Jesus, often ask to truly learn. In these situations, a wise answer can help remove barriers to belief.

Second, consider the heart. In chapter 4 we said that most Jesus-followers of Muslim backgrounds we know did not come to faith through apologetics. Instead they describe a process where *despite* their objections, their heart was warmed by the Christ they met through Scripture, prayer, and community, so that they wanted more and more of him. You might not convince your friends by your words, but the Spirit can still do his work in their hearts.

Third, consider your tone. Approach the topic as two people journeying to God, not two opponents facing off. Each of these responses aims not just to correct misunderstandings, but to promote deeper thinking. Each of these can lead to an invitation to read Scripture, so a great conclusion is "Why don't we read together so you can see for yourself?"

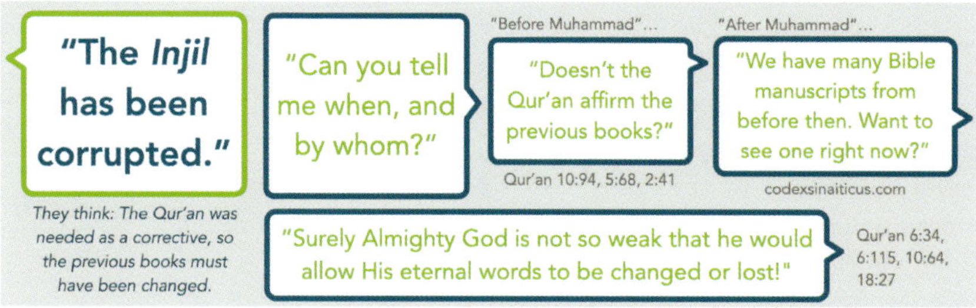

Most Muslim international students have been told that the *Injil*, Gospel–or the entire Bible–has been changed or lost to history. For some, this objection pops up the first time Scripture is mentioned. Others raise no disagreement with passages that do not conflict with their beliefs but raise objections later when the uniqueness of Christ is discussed.

Several verses in the Qur'an seem to speak of some type of corruption or change of holy books. Since the Qur'an claims to confirm the books that came before it, yet Islamic teaching differs in key ways from the biblical message, most Muslims infer that the previous books must have been changed at some point.

If a friend claims corruption *before* Muhammad, the natural question is why the Qur'an spends so much time affirming the *Injil* and *Tawrat*, Torah. Surely if these books were distorted, there would be severe warnings each time they are mentioned, but this is definitely not the case. Qur'an 10:94 instructs Muhammad to consult with Jews and Christians about God's revelation. "So if you are in doubt about that which We[77] have revealed to you, then ask those who have been reading the Scripture before you." There are multiple other examples: see Qur'an 2:285, 4:136, 5:68, 5:47, 2:41, 2:89, 2:91, 2:97, 2:101, 3:3, and 3:81.

Corruption *after* the time of Muhammad is highly implausible for two reasons. First, we have numerous partial and complete copies of the Bible from before the seventh century (the time of Muhammad) that confirm the same message we believe today. A simple internet search will provide many sources on this. Even if corrupted copies of Scripture have come about through the years, we can check them against early texts. One of the earliest is the Codex Sinaiticus, which dates from the mid-fourth century and can be read online (codexsinaiticus.com). You could open that site right then and there with your friend. For a helpful discussion of the manuscript evidence for the Bible, listen to the Theology in the Raw podcast, show #1014, October 6, 2022.

Second, by the seventh century the church had been established for hundreds of years and the Bible was available in a wide variety of languages and cultures across multiple continents. These churches differed on plenty of lesser theological topics, but they universally proclaimed that Jesus has risen from the dead, and is Lord and Savior, the two central claims of Christian Scripture. There is no plausible way that all existing Bible copies could have been replaced while all believers were duped in the process.

You might also point out that the accusation of Scripture corruption is an insult to God. Referring to God, Qur'an 6:34 says, "There is no substituting his words." Throughout our friends' holy book, this is a hallmark of God's greatness, so any accusation that he could allow his words to be lost to history denigrates him.

Finally, admit that Christians can certainly *misinterpret* or incorrectly teach what is in the text (cf. Qur'an 5:14-15). The best solution to this is to read the Bible, which is exactly what you and your friend should do!

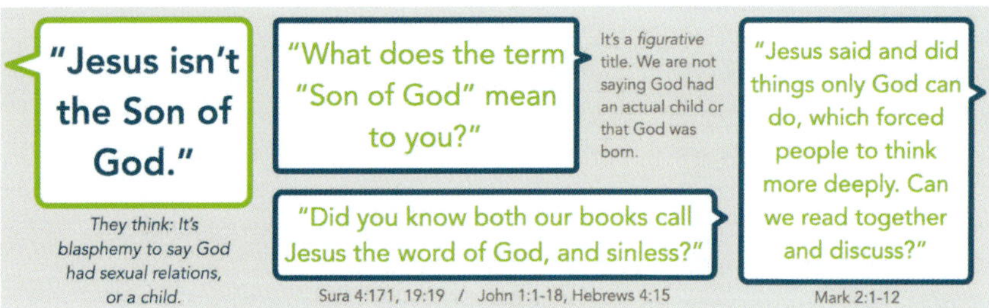

To Muslim ears, the words "Son of God" are offensive, even revolting. That is because in classical Arabic, 'son' and 'father' meant biological son and father. Within this framework, calling Jesus "son" implies that God had sexual relations leading to the birth of a child. This idea is every bit as revolting to Christians, so the first step is to remove the misunderstanding. Ask your friend what they understand by that term. Clarify we do not use it to describe a biological son and father, but figuratively.

Rather than arguing for the title "Son of God" from the outset with your Muslim friends, present the evidence in both the Qur'an and the Bible and invite them to draw a conclusion. The idea of divine sonship was difficult for first century Palestinian Jews to grasp, as well. Early followers became convinced that Jesus was more than a prophet and teacher by his unparalleled wisdom and miracles, by how he fulfilled prophecy, and ultimately by his resurrection.

The Qur'an attributes status and miracles to Jesus that exceed even Muhammad. Qur'an 4:171 says that "the Messiah, Isa son of Mariam, is Allah's messenger and his word which he sent down on Mariam, and a spirit from him." And in Qur'an 19:19 the angel told Mary/Mariam, "I am truly a messenger of your Lord to give you a sinless boy." (By comparison, Qur'an 48:2 mentions forgiveness for Muhammad's past and future sins.) It is appropriate to ask your friend, "How can such grand descriptions be given to a mere human?"

As you and your friends examine Jesus' life and words in the Bible, you will encounter direct statements about his divinity. In Matthew 1:23 the angel announces that "they will call him Immanuel (which means 'God with us')." In John 10:36-38 Jesus says, "the Father is in me, and I in the Father." And in Mark 2:1-12 Jesus claims the authority of God to forgive sins. Bowman and Komoszewski's *Putting Jesus in His Place: The Case for the Deity of Christ* documents how in the Bible, Jesus shares the honors due to God, the attributes of God, the names of God, the deeds that God does, and the seat of God's eternal throne.

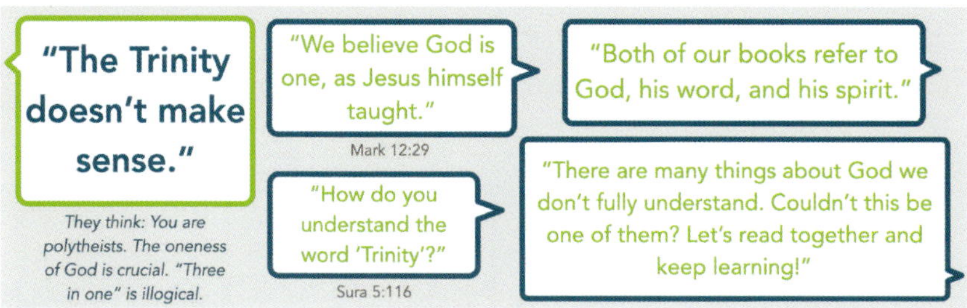

Muslims view any idea of God as three persons in one substance as polytheism. And it is extremely difficult to give a satisfactory explanation of the Trinity to a skeptical listener. It took the early church hundreds of years to hammer out their understanding of the triune God, and there is still disagreement over the details! The Trinity is not explicitly stated in the Bible, but an inference drawn from the text. The Bible depicts the Father, the Son, and the Spirit *each as divine*, while also expressing their *separateness*, while also stating that there is *one God.*

As with the deity of Christ, your first step is to correct a potential misunderstanding. Qur'an 5:116 states, "Isa, son of Mariam, did you tell the people: Take me and my mother as two gods in addition to Allah?" implying a trinity of God, Mary, and Jesus as three individual gods. This is unequivocally *not* Christian theology. We do not believe in three gods, and the Trinity is not made up of those three persons. Affirm Jesus' words in Mark 12:29 (quoting Deuteronomy 6:4): "Hear, O Israel: The Lord our God, the Lord is one."

Both the Qur'an and the Bible refer to God, his word, and his spirit, and Christians and Muslims have used these terms to attempt to understand each others' theology since the early centuries of Islam.[78] Your friend may not be aware that Islamic theologians have long debated among themselves how to understand the relationship between God's *essence* and his *attributes*, such as his knowledge, power, life, and word. The oneness of God, which we both believe in, is not as simple to describe as it seems on the surface. For a fascinating deep dive into this topic, see Cumming, *Ṣifāt al-Dhāt in Al-Ashʿarī's Doctrine of God and Possible Christian Parallels.*

Point out that God is unlike us and our words always fall short of describing him. Islamic apologists, whose ideas your friend has gleaned directly or indirectly, usually oversimplify the Trinity and then dismiss it as illogical. But it is hubris to dismiss an idea about God (and any evidence for it) simply because it is not easily understood. God is great, and our minds are limited (Psalm 139:1-18, Qur'an 2:255).

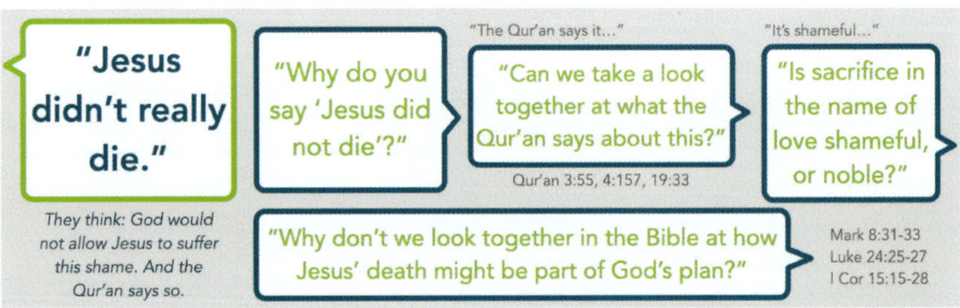

This objection is normally based on the idea that it would be shameful for a prophet to face the dishonor of death on a cross, so God would never allow Jesus to suffer in such a way. Later Islamic traditions, formed in an apologetic environment, tend to pave over contrary evidence both in the Qur'an and from the greatest classical Islamic scholars.

Four verses in the Qur'an are most pertinent to this objection. The first three imply an actual death of Jesus. In Qur'an 3:55 God says, "Isa, I will make you die and raise you up to me..." Many Qur'an translators use a word other than "die," but death is overwhelmingly the strongest translation of the word.[79] Qur'an 19:33 uses the same word for die, when the infant Jesus proclaims, "Peace be upon me the day I was born, the day I will die, and the day I will be resurrected alive!" And in Qur'an 5:117, Jesus, in conversation with God, refers to "when you made me die" and uses the same Arabic word.

The fourth pertinent verse is more ambiguous. Qur'an 4:157 says that the Jews did not kill Jesus, "but it seemed so to them." From this verse comes a common belief among Muslims that God replaced Jesus with Judas on the cross, yet made it appear that it was Jesus to onlookers. Some Islamic scholars reject this vehemently, as it makes God the author of deception.[80] In any case, the exact interpretation of the verse is unclear. Does it mean Jesus was not put to death *at all*, or that it was the *Romans* and not the Jews who did so, or that it was *God's* doing, or that he ultimately *rose* from the dead and so was not killed with finality?

What is fascinating is that the authors of the earliest, most respected, most popular and most famous Sunni commentaries on the Qur'an viewed these verses differently than contemporary Islamic apologists, as Cumming masterfully documents in "Did Jesus Die on the Cross? The History of Reflection on the End of His Earthly Life in Sunni Tafsir Literature." Mention the names Al-Tabarï, Al-Râzï, Al-Qurtubï, Al-Baydawi, and Sayyid Qutb. They are to Islam what Augustine, Aquinas, and Calvin are to Christianity. These Islamic scholars explained that there can be *multiple interpretations* of Qur'anic texts, and have the integrity to admit that Jesus' death (and even resurrection) are valid interpretations, whether they personally prefer them or not. Therefore, there is room for Muslims to accept the possibility that Christ died, so this objection should not stop them from investigating him.

▶ WHO IS JESUS THE MESSIAH?

Each passage in this Bible study series from the book of Luke draws out a different aspect of Jesus' message. Gradually, they reveal the fullness of his identity.

Read Luke 1:1-4 and 3:7-16 as an introduction.

Luke 4:14-21	Jesus defines his ministry to the least and left-out and names his coming as the fulfillment of Isaiah's prophecy 750 years prior.
Luke 5:1-11	Simon is amazed by the miraculous catch of fish, humbled before the power of the Messiah, and called into a new life following him.
Luke 5:17-32	Jesus claims the authority to forgive sins, then validates it by healing a paralyzed man. He socializes with known "sinners" and encourages all to admit our own need for him.
Luke 6:27-36	Jesus' command to "love your enemies" is challenging and an unmatched moral standard. It foreshadows the Messiah's sacrifice for sinners.
Luke 7:36-50	Jesus blesses and receives worship from a woman and makes her an example of faith while criticizing a self-righteous Pharisee. Again, readers are prodded to own our sin.
Luke 8:22-39	Jesus exercises authority over nature, then demons. Many Muslim cultures around the globe are familiar with cursing and demonism.
Luke 10:25-37	The Good Samaritan challenges us to love those who are not like us, and to demonstrate our faith through service. Choose a practical application with your friends.

Luke 11:1-13	Jesus teaches his disciples how to pray and describes God as a loving Father. The fatherhood of God is not in Islam, so this topic is both challenging and inviting.
Luke 12:22-31	In this passage Jesus teaches us to entrust our worries to him and seek God's kingdom as our first priority.
Luke 15:11-32	The parable of the two sons depicts two ways people rebel against God: hedonism in the younger son and legalism in the older. Both separate us from the Father's love, and both sons are graciously invited to enter the Father's joy.
Luke 18:9-14	Jesus' parable illustrates how our prayer and religious practice can become prideful. For an interesting twist, retell this story as two people in a mosque, and stop after verse 13 to ask your friend, "Which of the two do you think went home justified?"
Luke 19:28-40	The storyline focuses toward the cross with Jesus' triumphal entry into Jerusalem. The crowds welcome him, but they are looking for a political leader who will overthrow Rome's oppression. How often we try to conform God to our own ideas!
Luke 22:39-53	Many Muslims view the idea of Jesus dying as an insult and weakness. As we read his prayer and watch him willingly arrested, consider how humble sacrifice displays the Lord's tremendous love and strength.
Luke 22:66-23:5,26-49	Jesus shows his willingness to die as part of the divine plan and acknowledges his heavenly identity. On the cross he forgives a sinful man, blesses his enemies, and gives up his own life.
Luke 24:1-12, 36-53	Jesus rises from the dead, just as he said he would. On the Emmaus Road he explains that all the prophets foretold this astonishing event and then ascends to heaven.

▶ JESUS' INTERACTIONS WITH WOMEN

These stories display the Messiah's respect and care for women. Stories that occur in multiple Gospels are noted.

Matthew. 8:14-15, Mark 1:29-34, Luke 4:38-39	Jesus heals Peter's mother-in-law from her sickness, then many others.
John 4:6-30	Jesus talks to the Samaritan woman at the well and reveals himself as the Messiah to her.
Luke 7:11-17	Jesus comforts a widow after the loss of her son and then raises the son back to life.
Matthew 9:20-22, Mark 5:24-34, Luke 8:43-48	A woman who has suffered bleeding for twelve years is healed by Jesus, and he commends her faith.
Luke 7:36-50	Jesus receives worship from a sinful, repentant woman and forgives her sin. He honors her rather than a male religious teacher.
Luke 8:1-3	Jesus' followers included a number of women who have been healed by him.
Matthew 15:21-28; Mark 7:24-30	Jesus heals a Gentile woman's daughter and praises her faith.
John 8:3-11	Rather than join the religious leaders in stoning an adulterous woman, Jesus reminds them of their own sin, and the woman is saved.
Luke 10:38-42	Jesus visits two women, and praises the one who takes the place of a disciple and prioritizes learning from him.
John 11:1-46	Jesus mourns with two women whose brother has died. He is deeply moved, raises the man from the dead, and declares himself "the resurrection and the life."
Luke 13:10-17	Jesus heals a crippled woman on the Sabbath, demonstrating that people are more valuable than religious traditions.

Mark 12:41-44; Luke 21:1-4	A poor woman gives generously at the temple and Jesus praises her generosity over the giving of the rich.
Matthew 26:6-13; Mark 14:3-9	A woman anoints Jesus with expensive oil and Jesus defends her action to his disciples, calling it a beautiful deed.
Matthew 28:1-10; Mark 16:1-11; Luke 24:1-18	Mary Magdalene and Mary visit the tomb after Jesus' resurrection, and these women are the first witnesses of Jesus' resurrection.

▶ SHARED PROPHETS: A QUR'AN/BIBLE DISCUSSION GUIDE

Below is a summary of this scripture series, which examines seven prophets common to both our faiths, from Adam to Jesus. Through texts from both the Qur'an and the Bible, the stories of the prophets make clear that:

1. God himself provides the means for our salvation.
2. He does so through sacrifice.
3. Jesus, the Lamb of God, is the ultimate and final sacrifice for sin.

The full guide is available at tiny.cc/shared-prophets-guide.

In the story of Adam (also called Adam in the Qur'an) and Eve/Hawa eating from the tree against God's command, we see that there are serious consequences for sin. Yet God provided clothing from animal skin to cover their shame, physically and metaphorically.

The story of Noah/Nuh does not explicitly mention animal sacrifice, but again we see that *God* provided the means to be saved by inviting Noah to build and board the ark. There was no other way to escape judgment, and Noah obeyed the way of salvation God gave.

In the story of Abraham/Ibrahim, God graciously provided a ram as a blood sacrifice for Abraham and his son to offer God in worship. Though Abraham obeyed God, his obedience was not enough to save him. He needed to receive the sacrifice sent by God, which would die in place of his son.

In the story of Musa/Moses, God freed the people of Israel from literal slavery, which in the rest of Scripture is also viewed as a symbol of our greater problem, slavery to sin. At Passover those who were under the cover of the blood of the lamb were saved because the lamb had already been slain in their place. All who were not covered by the blood were subject to judgment.

The story of David/Dawud shows that even God-honoring prophets sin. David committed adultery, had a man killed, and hid his sin, but God knew. No one can attain God's standard of holiness, and like David, we all must confess our sin and ask God to grant us a clean heart. God also promised David that from his lineage would come the Messiah, the Savior, an anointed king with an eternal kingdom.

In the story of John the Baptist/Yahya, the prophet confirms a sign from God. John's ministry was preparing people to repent before the arrival of the promised Messiah. Then he identified Jesus as "the Lamb of God, who takes away the sin of the world" (John 1:29).

Finally, Jesus/Isa is the one called the Word of God and Messiah and the clear fulfillment of God's way of salvation seen through all the previous prophets. He exercised authority over demons, healed the sick, taught God's way with unparalleled insight, and is the only sinless one, ever. And in an astounding act of love, Jesus became the sacrifice—not animal skins, nor their blood, nor a ram, but he himself. His sacrifice fulfilled all earlier ones and was the final and complete answer to sin. And having laid down his life by his own choice, he raised it up to life again in victory!

Humans are deeply broken by sin, so much so that we need God's action to restore us—we cannot do it ourselves. The stories of the prophets point toward Jesus, the perfect sinless lamb, the ultimate sacrifice that redeems (literally saves from, exchanges, or pays for) our sin. We cannot ignore the signs God has given. We must receive Jesus, the sacrifice God has provided.

APPENDIX E FRIENDSHIPS WITH MUSLIM WOMEN (written by female campus ministers)

Muslim women on campus are very diverse. They arrive from different countries, have different understandings of Islam and practice varying levels of devotion. Some are confident and independent, while others are more dependent on their families, either by choice, cultural expectations, or strict obligation. In your friendship with a Muslim woman it is best to not make assumptions, and to get to know her for who *she* is: someone "fearfully and wonderfully made" (Psalm 139:14). (It is important to note that, in almost every case, it is best for women to befriend women.)

A REAL STORY

I befriended a Muslim art student, and since I was an illustrator, we began doing things together that involved art. We went to museums and collaborated on art projects. She helped me write my favorite Bible verses in Arabic calligraphy and then asked me questions about the verses. When we painted together, we talked about the character of God and his creation. These short "Bible studies" grew in consistency and length until she shared with me that she had had a dream about Isa coming to her and asking her to walk through his door to become a follower.

START WITH PRAYER

If you already have a friend on campus, pray now that God would provide opportunities to share Jesus with her. If you do not yet have a Muslim friend, pray that God would put someone in your path this week to befriend and then watch what God does!

WHERE TO MEET MUSLIM WOMEN

It is easy to meet Muslim women on campus. Consider places such as classes, the bus stop, a nearby shopping mall, coffee shops, or *halal* restaurants. You might also consider campus venues such as Muslim Student Union meetings, cultural clubs (e.g., Pakistani Students' Association), or English conversation groups. Take a risk to attend or introduce yourself and invite her out to coffee or tea.

MAKING A CONNECTION

Making a new friend can be awkward, and that's OK! Here are some ways to deepen the connection with your new friend.

- Start a simple conversation about her home, family, faith, and experiences in the US.
- Show interest in areas of her life by asking about her ideas of marriage, hopes and dreams, views and experiences of God, purpose in life, likes and dislikes.
- Find common interests and invite her to do something together such as practice English, do homework, talk about religion, go shopping, attend a movie, look at family photos, or visit a local landmark.
- Invite her to your home for tea or a meal to meet your family or roommates.

THINGS TO KNOW ABOUT MUSLIM WOMEN

- **Seeking Hope:** It is difficult to offer even simple generalizations due to the diversity of women on our campuses. It is important to grow our knowledge, however, because this is often an overlooked community. Many Muslim women feel hopeless about eternity, have been shamed as women, feel unloved by God, are insecure, and experience deep loneliness. You are a person with a message of hope.
- **Family:** The role of family is more important for Muslim women than it is for many American college students. This might look like living with

a male relative while at school, needing permission to attend certain activities, hosting family from overseas for lengthy visits, or staying in contact with family back home on a daily basis.

- **Appearance:** Not all Muslim women wear a *hijab* or other head covering. If your friend does, don't assume that she is submissive or oppressed. In fact, most Muslim women whom you will meet on campus are strong, highly educated, and free thinking. Also, appearance is a high cultural value and can determine or reflect their status in the community.
- **Trust:** The majority culture in America prizes individualism and therefore talks/thinks about giving respect or trust to an individual. In general, Muslims tend to extend trust as a community. When a friend trusts you, she will build your reputation within her whole community.
- **Friendship:** The idea of friendship differs in the US from many other places in the world. A friendship with a Muslim woman, particularly an international student, may be more intense than you are used to. Make space in your schedule and expectations so your friendship can flourish.
- **Spiritual Knowledge:** In a mixed group setting, Muslim women may defer to men to speak on spiritual topics. Women's religious training varies; in some cultures they are not given opportunities to study the Qur'an like their male counterparts. In other cultures, women are highly educated and eager to discuss theology.

WAYS TO BUILD TRUST

- Meet a practical need such as teaching her to drive, advocating for her needs, or interpreting American culture.
- Open up about your own life, including your struggles. Real relationships are two-way.
- Dress modestly. When possible, avoid clothing showing cleavage, wearing belly shirts or short shorts. When visiting her family, wear long tunic shirts and pants as a sign of respect.
- Ask permission before you post pictures of your friend online. She may want to curate her online image or avoid having men view her photos, or she may be concerned about safety.

WAYS TO DEVELOP SPIRITUAL CURIOSITY

- **Pray:** As bonds of trust grow, a friend may share about a trial she is experiencing. Show your concern by listening deeply and offering to pray for her. This may open a door to discuss your spiritual beliefs, prayer, the New Testament, and Jesus. Ask your friend if it is alright to pray in the way you are accustomed. If she says yes, then feel free to pray in the name of Jesus.
- **Tell Jesus Stories:** Connect stories from the Bible to situations in your life. Open up about your own relationship with Jesus and experiences of Christianity by weaving spirituality into conversations. Consider stories from Scripture about women (see appendix D).

Your friendships may seem costly at times, but loving Muslim women with thoughtfulness, care, and perseverance could change their lives. In fact, *you* may be the only Christian your friend ever gets to know. Be aware that Muslims may be in a relationship with a Christian friend for years before they begin to study God's Word or become a believer. Continue loving your friend and speaking about your faith, even if she doesn't seem to be interested in a Bible study. And continue to extend invitations for her to encounter Jesus. The Holy Spirit is in control of the timeline.

APPENDIX F GLOSSARY OF KEY TERMS

Ayat – Verse, in the Qur'an
Caliph – Muslim religious leader governing an Islamic state
Caliphate – Islamic state governed by a caliph
Dhimmi – A status for minority groups in an Islamic state, offering certain protections as well as restrictions.
Hadith – Collections of texts containing stories from Muhammad's life
Halal – Acceptable by Islamic custom
Haram – Forbidden by Islamic custom
Hijra – Muhammad's migration from Mecca to Medina; year one of the Islamic calendar
Hutba – The sermon given after midday prayers on Friday, at *jumma*
Iftar – The fast-breaking meal eaten at sunset during Ramadan, traditionally begun by eating dates
Imam – A person who leads prayers in a mosque
Injil – Gospel
Inshallah – God-willing, or "If God wills it."
Isa al Masih – Jesus the Messiah
Jibril – The angel Gabriel

Jinn – Spirit beings in Islam that bring good and bad but are commonly associated with oppressing and cursing people

Jumma – The high point of the Islamic week, Friday midday, with prayer and a *hutba*, sermon

Mahdi – Messianic figure in Islamic eschatology, though understood differently by Sunni and Shi'a

MSA/MSU – The Muslim Student Association/Union, a campus student organization

Mujahideen – Soldiers fighting for Islamic causes

Persia – An empire from the 6th to 20th centuries, the historical precursor to modern-day Iran. "Persian" is sometimes used to describe Iranian people and culture.

Ramadan – The ninth month of the Muslim year, during which strict fasting is observed from sunrise to sunset

Shah – A king of Iran

Shahada – The Muslim declaration of faith: "There is no god but God, and Muhammad is the messenger of god"

Sharia – Islamic law

Shi'a – The smaller of the two main branches of Islam, comprising approximately 15% of the world's Muslims, that rejects the first three Sunni caliphs and regards Ali, the fourth caliph, as Muhammad's first true successor.

Sufi – A Muslim ascetic and mystic

Sultan – The sovereign ruler of a Muslim state

Sunni – The larger of the two main branches of Islam, comprising approximately 85% of the world's Muslims. Sunnis differ from Shi'as in how they understand Muslim law and tradition, in how they exercise religious leadership, and in having accepted the first three caliphs after Muhammed's death.

Sura – Chapter in the Qur'an

Tawrat – Torah, the first five books of the Hebrew Scripture: Genesis, Exodus, Leviticus, Numbers, and Deuteronomy; also known as the Pentateuch

Umma – The global community of Islam, comprising all Muslims

Zabur – The Bible's Psalms and wisdom literature

NOTES

1 FOLLOWING JESUS' EXAMPLE

1. *Halal*, the Arabic word for "permissible," denotes foods (and other practices) that are acceptable in Islam. *Haram*, "forbidden," is the opposite.
2. IVP New Bible Dictionary, 3rd ed. (Downers Grove: InterVarsity Press,1999), s.v. "Samaritans."
3. Dallas Jenkins, *The Chosen*, "Woman at the Well," 2017, video, youtube.com/watch?v=f_UNAQFRhBY.

2 ACKNOWLEDGING MUSLIM-CHRISTIAN HISTORY

4. Tamin Ansary, *Destiny Disrupted: A History of the World through Islamic Eyes*, xvii.
5. Notre Dame professor Gabriel Said Reynolds' *The Emergence of Islam: Classical Traditions in Contemporary Perspective* is a good place to dig deeper into the origins discussion.
6. This is the common belief of most Muslims but has been debated due to multiple meanings of the Arabic word. See footnote 1318, p.193 in the *Reference Qur'an* v.4.2, 2016.
7. Vince Bantu's *A Multitude of All Peoples: Engaging Ancient Christianity's Global Identity* gives a fascinating account of the diverse expressions of Christianity across the Middle East, Asia, and Africa.
8. All Qur'anic references are from the *Reference Qur'an*, 2016. Note that in this interpretation of the Qur'an, verse numbers follow the verses. They do not precede them as most Bible readers are used to.
9. See chapter 3.
10. For more examples of the Qur'an validating the Torah and the Gospels see suras 4:136, 2:136, 5:59, 29:45-46, 5:47, 10:94, 2:285.
11. Reynolds points out, "However, the notion of Meccan and Medinan suras is nowhere found in the Qur'an itself" but comes from later commentators, 91.
12. See chapter 3.
13. Sydney Griffith, *The Church in the Shadow of the Mosque*, 11.
14. These descriptions of life in the caliphate come from Hugh Goddard, *A History of Christian-Muslim Relations*, and Griffith. Dhimmitude is a complex topic. Middle Eastern scholar Martin Accad said, "The *dhimmi* status historically was essentially a Muslim legal concept of 'protection of minorities.' Linguistically, when you are in someone's *dhimma*, you are under their care and protection. Of course, as we know, this did lead

to second class citizenship, but not so much because Muslims wanted to subdue Christians but because being under someone's protection is patronizing and infantilizing. But this latter understanding is modern. In those days, being under someone's *dhimma* in a patronage system was a good place to be." (Accad, personal email conversation with author), September 2, 2022).

15. This was a departure from the polemical style of Greek-speaking Western Christians, as explained in David Vila, "Arab Christians and Islam: Conflicts and Contributions," in *Christian Scholar's Review,* 2005, 4.
16. The works of Abu Ra'ita, Abu Qurra, and Ammar al-Basri are described in Griffith, *The Church in the Shadow of the Mosque*; Mark Beaumont, "Christology in Dialogue with Muslims: A Critical Analysis of Christian Presentation of Christ for Muslims from the Ninth and Twentieth Centuries" in *Regnum Studies in Mission,* 2011; and Mark Swanson, "The Trinity in Christian-Muslim Conversation," in *Dialog,* 2005, 256-263.
17. Beaumont, xxii.
18. Timothy's example is related by John Coakley and Andrea Sterk, *Readings in World Christian History,* and Khalid Samir, "The prophet Muhammed as seen by Timothy 1 and other Arab Christian Authors" in *Syrian Christians under Islam.*
19. Parshall, "Contextualization," in *Toward Respectful Understanding and Witness among Muslims: Essays in Honor of J. Dudley Woodberry,* ed. Evelyne Reisacher, 231.
20. Guibert de Nogent, *The Deeds of God Through the Franks,*131, google.com/books/edition/The_Deeds_of_God_Through_the_Franks/RTu6KGKtWGoC?hl=en&gbpv=1&bsq=sepulchre.
21. Dale Irvin and Scott Sunquist, *History of the World Christian Movement,* vol. 1, *Earliest Christianity to 1453,* 395-404.
22. Goddard, 91.
23. Paul Moses, *The Saint and the Sultan: The Crusades, Islam, and Francis of Assisi's Mission of Peace,* and gordonconwell.edu/blog/damietta-francis-and-the-sultan/, accessed 8/25/22.
24. Jehu Hanciles, *Beyond Christendom: Globalization, African Migration, and the Transformation of the West,* 101.
25. Kazakh and Kyrgyz friends have told me that in Central Asia, Jesus (in the Christian understanding of him) is dismissed by Muslims as "the Russian god."
26. Irvin and Sunquist, *History of the World Christian Movement,* vol. 2, *Modern Christianity from 1454 to 1800,* 3.
27. Today the majority of the world's Christians reside outside the West. Our faith truly is global, but the perception of Christianity as a Western religion remains. It may be that this will gradually change in the future, and to that end we can pray for Christian leaders from around the world to be recognized and grow in influence.

28. Sadrach's story was researched by Sutarman Partonadi, *Sadrach's Community and its Contextual Roots: A Nineteenth Century Javanese Expression of Christianity.*
29. Partonadi, 101.
30. This description of Sadrach's church comes from Parshall.
31. Parshall, 222.
32. A colleague in Southeast Asia said Christians there consider it both a heroic example of local faith and theologically confusing.
33. Ansary, xv.
34. For further reading on this topic see Munther Isaac, *The Other Side of the Wall: A Palestinian Christian Narrative of Lament and Hope* and Gary Burge, *Whose Land? Whose Promise?: What Christians are not Being Told about Israel and the Palestinians.*
35. news.un.org/en/story/2020/12/1078972, accessed 8/29/22.
36. Meic Pearse, *Why the Rest Hates the West,* 31-32.
37. history.com/this-day-in-history/cia-assisted-coup-overthrows-government-of-iran and britannica.com/biography/Mohammad-Reza-Shah-Pahlavi, both accessed 9/1/22.

3 UNDERSTANDING MUSLIM INTERNATIONAL STUDENTS

38. Interestingly, a number of Islamic scholars reject—or find problems with—the theory of scripture corruption. See chapter 5 and appendix C for more on this topic.
39. quraninalllanguages.com, accessed 8/31/22.
40. Huda, "The Importance of the Arabic Language," *Learn Religions,* https://www.learnreligions.com/arabic-language-in-islam-2004035; encounteringislam.org/muslim-world-facts, both accessed 8/31/22.
41. In truth, Christians also believe in salvific judgment on the final day. The difference is the basis upon which we are judged. For all who trust Christ, judgment will be based not on our *own* record of deeds but on His perfect obedience. So the apostle Paul can say in Romans 8 that "in Christ Jesus" we are already children of God, heirs, justified, and certain to be glorified.
42. Woodberry convincingly demonstrated that these pillars of Islam "are all adaptations of previous Jewish and Christian forms." This includes the statement of faith, prayer postures and at fixed times, ablutions (washing before prayer), giving alms, fasting, and pilgrimage. His point was that Christians can freely engage with and contextualize these forms. See J. Dudley Woodberry, "Contextualizing Using Common Pillars," *The Word Among Us: Contextualizing Theology for Mission Today,* ed. Gililand Dean, 282-312.
43. David Garrison's book, *A Wind in the House of Islam: How God is Drawing Muslims around the World to faith in Jesus Christ,* broadens this to nine "rooms" or regions and describes how the Spirit is moving through each.

44. In recent decades it increasingly makes sense to identify Europe and North America as one more corner of the Islamic world, with its own perspectives increasingly shaped by democracy, individualism, and progressive thinking.
45. John Esposito, *What Everyone Needs to Know about Islam*, 2nd ed., 48.
46. Thomas Finger, "Waiting for the Mahdi," *Christian Century*. June 17, 2008, 27.
47. In 2014, Bradley named a conservative estimate of 370,000 and a high estimate of 700,000. Mark Bradley, *Too Many to Jail*, 25.
48. Martin Goldsmith, "Community and Controversy: Key Causes of Muslim Resistance," *Missiology* 4, no.3, July 1976, 318.
49. There is much more to learn about honor and shame. Two solid resources are Jayson Georges' *The 3D Gospel: Ministry in Guilt, Shame, and Fear Cultures*, and Werner Mischke's *The Global Gospel*.
50. Sahih al-Bukhari 9:87:144.
51. Popular practices, also called folk Islam, contrast with formal Islam. Formal Islam refers to the proper beliefs described in the first half of this chapter. Popular Islam refers to the rituals and practices pragmatic Muslims do to deal with everyday struggles and concerns. This includes a wide variety of power objects, times, people, places, and rituals. Western Christians often have an underdeveloped awareness of the spiritual world and so are unprepared to respond to our friends' felt needs. (Cf. Caleb Kim, John Travis, and Anna Travis, "Relevant Responses to Folk Muslims," in *Seed to Fruit: Global Trends, Fruitful Practices, and Emerging Issues among Muslims*, 239-249, and Paul Hiebert, "The Flaw of the Excluded Middle" in *Missiology: An International Review*, Vol. X, No. 1, 1982, 35-47.)

4 BUILDING GOSPEL FRIENDSHIPS

52. This is not to say that there is no place for apologetics, but that they go better after you have built trust together. Seekers will have to navigate through many of these topics on the journey to faith. For that reason, appendix C discusses a variety of thorny issues.
53. Chesterton took part in a newspaper survey on "What's wrong with the world today?" His answer: "Dear sir, I am."
54. Sobhi Malek, *Introduction to Islam*, 4th ed., 288.
55. Sahih al-Bukhari, Chapter 5, Number 6990.
56. Katie Rawson, *Crossing Cultures with Jesus*, 48.
57. See chapter 2 in Katie Rawson's *Crossing Cultures with Jesus*, and Charles Kraft's *Deep Wounds, Deep Healing* to learn more about exercising spiritual authority in prayer.
58. Lamin Sanneh, *Disciples of All Nations: Pillars of World Christianity*, 1st ed., 2007.
59. Sanneh, 25, 56.

5 READING SCRIPTURE

60. See also multilanguagemedia.org.
61. Note that David says his sin is a direct affront to God. Most Muslims believe sin cannot affect God since he is wholly transcendent. But seeing the prophet *Dawud* confess this challenges their thinking.
62. Like Christians, Muslims believe that God provided an animal. But exactly *what* was sacrificed is not mentioned in the Qur'an. We need the Bible's account in Genesis 22:1-14 to learn that it was a ram and so to complete the story.

6 HELPING FRIENDS BECOME FOLLOWERS

63. Listening prayer is the practice of quieting before God to allow Him to give love and guidance. It can be practiced alone or in community. Here is a suggested process for listening prayer with a Muslim friend:

    Open by praising God and thanking him for the opportunity to draw near in prayer.

    Name the thing you seek God's guidance for. It could be a friend's physical or emotional need, or a barrier to belief in Jesus, or a desire to know Christ more.

    Ask God to send a word, image or other expression of his love, then wait in silence for several minutes.

    After waiting, ask your friend if they sensed anything that may be from God. Share anything you sensed. Know that God will always speak in accord with His revealed Word, the Bible.

    Pray in response to what you heard.

    If you did not sense any word or image from the Lord, try listening again. It is ok not to hear anything. You can always pray words of Scripture over your friend.
64. John Stott, Christian Mission in the Modern World. 2008, 168-171, quoted in Warrick Farah, "Emerging Missiological Themes in MBB Conversion Factors," *IJFM* 30:1. 2013, 14.
65. Tim Keller, "The Gospel in All its Forms," *Christianity Today International/ Leadership Journal.* Spring 2008, Vol. XXIX, No. 2.
66. The inspiration for this approach comes from "The Straight Path Timeline" by Common Ground Consultants.
67. Nabeel Qureshi, *Seeking Allah, Finding Jesus: A Devout Muslim Encounters Christianity.*

7 WALKING WITH NEW BELIEVERS

68. Full quote: "Religion operates on the principle of 'I obey—therefore I am accepted by God.' The basic operating principle of the gospel is 'I am

accepted by God through the work of Jesus Christ—therefore I obey.'" Keller, *The Prodigal God,* p.128.

69. Hiebert, Paul. "Critical Contextualization," 287-296.
70. Rawson, 50.
71. Kraft, 212.
72. opendoorsusa.org/christian-persecution/world-watch-list, accessed 12/21/21. Additionally, the world's top ten most populous Muslim countries are all on the World Watch list.
73. Nik Ripken, *The Insanity of Obedience: Walking with Jesus in Tough Places,* 105-111.
74. Accad, personal conversation, June 2018.
75. Nik Ripken and Barry Stricker, "Muslim Background Believers and Baptism in Cultures of Persecution and Violence," January 2006, accessed 9/8/22, https://www.nikripken.com/wp-content/themes/nikripken/downloads/Muslim%20Background%20Believers%20and%20Baptism%20in%20Cultures%20of%20Persecution%20and%20Violence.pdf.

8 PREPARING FOR REENTRY

76. Get copies of Lisa Espineli Chinn's *Think Home* workbook for your international students to help them work through reverse culture shock and other adjustments needed for returning home. Available at tiny.cc/t-home from the InterVarsity Store.

APPENDIX C: TURNING OBJECTIONS INTO GOOD CONVERSATIONS

77. The Qur'an regularly uses the royal "we" for God. This does not imply that God is a multiplicity, like a Trinity.
78. See Beaumont, 2005, 195-203 and Beaumont, 2011, 15-65.
79. Reference Qur'an, footnote 532 says: "This word in Arabic /tawaffa/ means "to cause to die." Some translators ignore the clear statement of the Qur'an that Isa died, and instead translate common beliefs. The clearest commentary on the Qur'an is the Qur'an itself, not what others say about it. This verb, in its various forms, occurs 25 times in the Qur'an. Twice (here and 5:117) it refers to Isa, and everywhere else (2:234,240, 3:193, 4:15,97, 6:60,61, 7:37,126, 8:50, 10:46,104, 12:101, 13:40, 16:28,32,70, 22:5, 32:11, 39:42, 40:67,77, 47:27), it is in the context of death. Even today, it is used euphemistically to mean "to pass away," and the word "obituaries" is from the same root. For other verses which state or imply Isa's death, see 5:117, 19:33, 19:31, 2:87, etc."
80. Joseph Cumming, "Did Jesus Die on the Cross?" 17, 27.